VIVA
Bloom's
NOTES

Zora Neale Hurston's

THEIR EYES WERE WATCHING GOD

VIVA
Bloom's
NOTES

Zora Neale Hurston's

THEIR EYES WERE WATCHING GOD

Edited and with an Introduction by

HAROLD BLOOM

Viva Books Private Limited
New Delhi • Mumbai • Chennai • Kolkata • Bangalore • Hyderabad

First Indian Edition 2007

VIVA BOOKS PRIVATE LIMITED

- 4737/23 Ansari Road, Daryaganj, New Delhi 110 002
  E-mail: vivadelhi@vivagroupindia.net, Tel. 42242200

- Plot No. 76, Service Industries, Shirvane, Sector 1, Nerul, Navi Mumbai 400 706
  E-mail: vivamumbai@vivagroupindia.net, Tel. 27721273, 27721274

- Jamals Fazal Chambers, 26 Greams Road, Chennai 600 006
  E-mail: vivachennai@vivagroupindia.net, Tel. 28290304, 28294241

- B-103, Jindal Towers, 21/1A/3 Darga Road, Kolkata 700 017
  E-mail: vivakolkata@vivagroupindia.net, Tel. 22836381, 22816713

- 7, Sovereign Park Apartments, 56-58, K. R. Road, Basavanagudi, Bangalore 560 004
  E-mail: vivabangalore@vivagroupindia.net, Tel.26607409, 26607410

- 101-102 Mughal Marc Apartments, 3-4-637 to 641, Narayanguda, Hyderabad 500 029
  E-mail: vivahyderabad@vivagroupindia.net, Tel. 27564481, 27564482

Published by arrangement with

Facts on File, Inc.
132 West 31st Street
New York NY 10001
USA

ISBN 81-309-0731-3

Published by Vinod Vasishtha for Viva Books Private Limited, 4737/23 Ansari Road
New Delhi 110 002. Printed and bound at Anand Sons, Delhi.

Contents

User's Guide 6

Editor's Note 7

Introduction 9

Biography of Zora Neale Hurston 11

Thematic and Structural Analysis 13

List of Characters 25

Critical Views

Richard Wright: The Minstrel Tradition and the Novel 27
Robert Bone: The Role of Suffering in the Novel 28
Arthur P. Davis: Hurston's View of Race Relations in the Novel 31
Ann L. Rayson: The Life-Affirming Qualities of the Novel 32
S. Jay Walker: Hurston's Version of Feminism 35
Robert E. Hemenway: Janie's Quest for Self-Discovery 37
Alice Walker: The Emotional Potency of the Novel 41
Maria Tai Wolff: Symbolism of the Opening Passage of the Novel 43
Cyrena N. Pondrom: Mythology and Tea Cake 46
Karla F.C. Holloway: Narrative Technique in the Novel 49
Klaus Benesch: The Role of "Black English" in the Novel 51
Henry Louis Gates Jr.: Narrative Structure of the Novel 53
John F. Callahan: Hurston's *Mules and Men* and the Novel 56
Nellie McKay: The Autobiographical Content of the Novel 59
Rachel Blau DuPlessis: Hurston's Use of the Court Trial Metaphor 61
Mary Helen Washington: The Language of the Novel 64
Phillipa Kafka: Gender Roles in the Novel 65
Dolan Hubbard: The Mythology of the Black Sermon 67
Kimberly Rae Connor: Janie's Guides Toward Self-Awareness 70
John Lowe: Freud's Concept of Humor as Aggression in the Novel 72

Works by Zora Neale Hurston 76

Works About Zora Neale Hurston and *Their Eyes Were Watching God* 77

Index of Themes and Ideas 80

User's Guide

This volume is designed to present biographical, critical, and bibliographical information on the author and the work. Following Harold Bloom's editor's note and introduction are a detailed biography of the author, discussing major life events and important literary works. Then follows a thematic and structural analysis of the work, which traces significant themes, patterns, and motifs. An annotated list of characters supplies brief information on the chief characters in the work.

A selection of critical extracts, derived from previously published material by leading critics, then follows. The extracts consist of statements by the author, early reviews of the work, and later evaluations up to the present. These items are arranged chronologically by date of first publication. A bibliography of the author's writings (including a complete list of all books written, cowritten, edited, and translated), a list of additional books and articles on the author and the work, and an index of themes conclude the volume.

Harold Bloom is Sterling Professor of the Humanities at Yale University and Henry W. and Albert A. Berg Professor of English at the New York University Graduate School. He is the author of twenty books and the editor of more than thirty anthologies of literary criticism.

Professor Bloom's works include *Shelley's Mythmaking* (1959), *The Visionary Company* (1961), *Blake's Apocalypse* (1963), *Yeats* (1970), *A Map of Misreading* (1975), *Kabbalah and Criticism* (1975), and *Agon: Towards a Theory of Revisionism* (1982). *The Anxiety of Influence* (1973) sets forth Professor Bloom's provocative theory of the literary relationships between the great writers and their predecessors. His most recent books include *The American Religion* (1992), *The Western Canon* (1994), and *Omens of Millennium: The Gnosis of Angels, Dreams, and Resurrection* (1996).

Professor Bloom earned his Ph.D. from Yale University in 1955 and has served on the Yale faculty since then. He is a 1985 MacArthur Foundation Award recipient and served as the Charles Elkot Norton Professor of Poetry at Harvard University in 1987–88. He is currently the editor of other Chelsea House series in literary criticism, including MAJOR LITERARY CHARACTERS, MODERN CRITICAL VIEWS, and WOMEN WRITERS OF ENGLISH AND THEIR WORKS.

Editor's Note

My Introduction reflects upon both Zora Neale Hurston and Janie Crawford, finding in both an heroic vitalism that quests for the Blessing, in its true Biblical sense of "more life."

The Critical Extracts commence with the pioneering African-American novelist, Richard Wright, who rather strangely finds in Hurston's characters America's racist stereotype of its black citizens: "between laughter and tears." Robert Bone more appreciatively considers Janie's tragic intensity, while Arthur P. Davis suggests that Hurston's portraits of white good will seem incredible to many blacks.

In Ann L. Rayson's view, Hurston exemplifies a zest for life, but S. Jay Walker regards *Their Eyes Were Watching God* as being a sexist work. A very different argument is made by Robert E. Hemenway, who rightly (in my judgment) finds in Janie Crawford a persuasive portrait of a liberated black woman, always aware of her own need for self-fulfillment and the obstacles it must overcome.

The novelist Alice Walker, who claims Hurston as precursor, compares her to great black female singers, while Maria Tai Wolff emphasizes Janie's transformative power.

Tea Cake, Janie's tragic lover, is judged by Cyrena M. Pondrom to be a properly mythic consort for Hurston's heroine, after which Karla F.C. Holloway praises the novel's narrative skill.

Klaus Benesch asserts that Black English is Hurston's linguistic medium, while the most illustrious African-American critic, H.L. Gates Jr., studies the "structure of exchange" in *Their Eyes Were Watching God*.

The storyteller's voice in Hurston is the concern of John F. Callahan, after which Nellie McKay emphasizes the autobiographical element in the novel, and Rachel Blau DuPlessis sees the books as having the structure of a court trial.

Mary Helen Washington believes that *Their Eyes Were Watching God* has helped revised a male-dominated literary canon, while Phillipa Kafka interprets the novel through aspects of Hurston's life story, and Dolan Hubbard reads Janie's struggle as a version of the African American church sermon.

Janie's growth in awareness of self is traced by Kimberly Rae Connor, and then John Lowe concludes this volume by applying Freud's theory of humor to the comic elements in *Their Eyes Were Watching God*.

Introduction

HAROLD BLOOM

Rereading *Their Eyes Were Watching God* after a decade away from it remains a satisfying aesthetic experience, simplistic as the novel sometimes appears to be. Its alternation of poignancy and humor has something of a folk-tale effectiveness, and even a Biblical flavor, based partly upon its sermon-like directness. Zora Neale Hurston, a superbly flamboyant personality, bestows aspects of her own exuberance upon the indomitable Janie Crawford. Herself anything but an ideologue, Hurston would be amused by much of the doctrinal rant that her novel has aroused in the "cultural critics" who now crowd out what once was termed "literary study." *Their Eyes Were Watching God* is in no way tendentious; it does not seek to raise the flag of Liberation for black women. Like Hurston herself, Janie's quest is for what the Bible called the Blessing: more life into a time without boundaries. Such a search for self-fulfillment is universal; it does not belong to any gender, any race, any particular mode of belief or skepticism. The perpetual freshness of *Their Eyes Were Watching God* ensues from Hurston's breakthrough into a narrative strong and poised enough to transcend its immediate social contexts. Doubtless, the book, like any other can be put to what use you will, but it remains a pleasure to read, and ultimately must survive as such.

For women, Hurston begins by observing: "The dream is the truth." That observation is more a defiance than an irony, or ironically is a defiance directed primarily against Janie's grandmother, Nanny, whose thwarted ambition both for Janie's mother and for Janie, was to help them avoid the destiny of the black woman: to be "the mule of the world." Nanny's dream alienated Janie's mother, and compelled Janie herself into two absurdly bad marriages. "A cracked plate," Nanny calls herself, and she cannot prevent Janie from the tragic joy of her superb relationship to Tea Cake, her true companion and lover.

Haunted by the light of the sun's vitality, Janie's last vision of Tea Cake, whom she had to slay when he became murderously insane, is: "Tea Cake, with the sun for a shawl."

Hurston was both a mythologist and a vitalist, and her self-image is reflected in Janie's heroism. More profoundly, Janie exemplifies Hurston's authentic religion, an African-American gnosticism that goes back to the early black Baptists with their African concept of "the little me within the big me." That "little me" is the gnostic spark, the best and oldest part of the self, and like God no part of the Creation-Fall:

> When God had made the Man, he made him out of stuff that sung all the time and glittered all over. Then after that some angels got jealous and chopped him into millions of pieces, but still he glittered and hummed. So they beat him down to nothing but sparks, but each spark had a shine and a song. So they covered each one over with mud. And the lonesomeness in the sparks made them hunt for one another, but the mud is deaf and dumb. Like all the other tumbling mud-balls, Janie had tried to show her shine.

Hurston's spirit, and Janie's, is with us still in the poetry of Thylias Moss, where the gnosis of an heroic vision prevails, in continuity with *Their Eyes Were Watching God*. ✣

Biography of Zora Neale Hurston

(1891–1960)

Zora Neale Hurston was born probably on January 7, 1891, although she frequently gave her birth date as 1901 or 1903. She was born and raised in America's first all-black incorporated town, Eatonville, Florida. Her father, John Hurston, was a former sharecropper who became a carpenter, preacher, and three-term mayor of Eatonville. Her mother, Lucy Hurston, died in 1904; two weeks after her death, Hurston was sent to Jacksonville, Florida, to school, but wound up neglected by her remarried father and worked a variety of menial jobs. A five-year gap in her personal history at this time has led some biographers to conjecture that she was married; however, no evidence exists to support or disprove this speculation. In 1917 she began studies at Morgan Academy in Baltimore and in 1918 attended Howard University, where her first short story appeared in the college literary magazine. She later won a scholarship to Barnard College to study with the eminent anthropologist Franz Boas.

While living in New York Hurston worked as a secretary to the popular novelist Fannie Hurst. Though she only lived in New York for a short time, Hurston is considered a major force in the Harlem Renaissance of the 1920s and 1930s. She was an associate editor for the one-issue avante-garde journal *Fire!!* and she collaborated on several plays with various writers, including *Mule Bone: A Comedy of Negro Life*, written with Langston Hughes. Boas arranged a fellowship for Hurston that allowed her to travel throughout the South and collect folklore. The result of these travels was the publication of Hurston's first collection of black folktales, *Mules and Men* (1935). Hurston is thought to be the first black American to have collected and published Afro-American folklore, and both of her collections have become much used sources for myths and legends of black culture. Her interest in anthropology took her to several

Latin American countries, including Jamaica, Haiti, and Honduras. Her experiences in Jamaica and Haiti appear in her second collection of folktales, *Tell My Horse* (1938).

Hurston's first novel, *Jonah's Gourd Vine* (1934), is loosely based on the lives of her parents in Eatonville. It was written shortly after *Mules and Men* (although it was published first) and has been criticized as being more of an anthropological study than a novel. Her best-known work, the novel *Their Eyes Were Watching God*, was published in 1937. Written after a failed love affair, *Their Eyes Were Watching God* focuses on a middle-aged woman's quest for fulfillment in an oppressive society. Hurston also wrote *Moses, Man of the Mountain* (1939), an attempt to fuse biblical narrative and folk myth. In addition to her life as a writer, Hurston worked temporarily as a teacher, a librarian at an air force base, a staff writer at Paramount Studios, and a reporter for the *Fort Pierce* [*Florida*] *Chronicle*.

Her autobiography, *Dust Tracks on a Road*, won the 1943 Annisfield Award. Her final novel, *Seraph on the Suwanee*, appeared in 1948. An attempt to universalize the issues addressed in *Their Eyes Were Watching God*, *Seraph* is Hurston's only novel to feature white protagonists. Hurston's other honors include Guggenheim Fellowships in 1936 and 1938. She wrote for various magazines in the 1950s, but her increasingly conservative views concerning race relations effectively alienated her from black intellectual culture. She died on January 28, 1960, in Fort Pierce, Florida. ♣

Thematic and Structural Analysis

The **first chapter** of Zora Neale Hurston's *Their Eyes Were Watching God* begins with a description of the text as a figuration of male struggle: "Ships at a distance have every man's wish on board. For some they come in with the tide. For others they sail forever on the horizon, never out of sight, never landing until the Watcher turns his eyes away in resignation, his dreams mocked to death by Time. That is the life of men." In a different, less metaphorical, voice we confront Hurston's answer to this voice, the construction of a female authorial and narrative voice: "Now, women forget all those things they don't want to remember, and remember everything they don't want to forget. The dream is the truth. Then they act and do things accordingly." The story begins. As if to confirm this refiguration of the male text "a woman" returns from burying "the bloated; the sudden dead" at "the beginning of this," a woman's story. In black dialect and lush metaphor Hurston's narrative evokes an idea of the black woman as individual and as storyteller.

Described through the critical eyes and mouths of a Florida town (a black community called Eatonville, as we will later learn) the protagonist, Janie Starks, is forty years old; she had left town in a blue satin dress; her husband had died and was presumed to have left her money; she had taken up with another man (all wonder what *he* did with her money); and she refuses to "stay in her class." Phoeby Watson brings Janie a dinner of "mulatto rice;" they have been friends since Janie came to Eatonville. Although Hurston has been criticized by many modern black critics and writers for her use of what is called black English, the dialect creates for the reader an intimacy reserved only for the closest of friends. Overhearing the conversation between Janie and Phoeby we are initiated into the novel's world. Janie reveals to us that she has been gone a year and a half, and to Phoeby that "Tea Cake is gone. . . . Down in the Everglades there, down on the muck." The women sit on Janie's back porch and Janie tells her story to Phoeby.

In the **second chapter** the novel reveals itself to be a *Bildungsroman*, a story about one's passage from childhood to maturity. We see events primarily through Janie's eyes. Janie "saw her life like a great tree in leaf with the things suffered, things enjoyed, things done and undone. Dawn and doom was in the branches." The *motif* of the tree, a recurrent thematic element, will recur throughout the novel.

Janie was raised by Nanny, her grandmother, first in the home of Nanny's white employer, and later, in a house Nanny buys. In this chapter Janie recalls two events that define her childhood. The first concerns a photograph; the second, a first kiss. Janie is photographed with a group of white children and she cannot see herself in the finished picture. "Dat's you, Alphabet, don't you know yo' ownself?" a white women laughs. For Janie, the realization that she is "colored," and not "just like de rest" is an *epiphany*, a profound revelation that changes her stance toward the world. Her "colored" schoolmates tease her about "livin' in de white folks backyard" and refuse to play with her, so Nanny buys a house and land for the two of them.

"Shiftless" Johnny Taylor comes later, transformed by her youthful perceptions, ("the golden dust of pollen had beglamored his rags and her eyes") she kisses him. She names this moment the beginning of her "conscious life." Nanny sees the boy "lacerating her Janie with a kiss" and knows that she is no longer the strongest influence in Janie's life; she is like a "[f]oundation of ancient power that no longer mattered." We may interpret this enigmatic allusion in many ways. Most immediately it suggests that the power of a mother to protect her daughter—or a grandmother her granddaughter—ends when the girlchild turns to the world of men, outside the home where the old woman "no longer matter[s]." Nanny insists that seventeen-year-old Janie marry a prosperous but dull farmer, Logan Killicks, who will protect her from the vulnerabilities of her gender and class. But, she tells Janie, even Logan will not protect her from some things, now that she has left Nanny's home. Nanny offers a parable about a further division of gender within race: "De nigger woman is de mule uh de world so fur as Ah can see. Ah been prayin' fuh it tuh be different wid you." A former slave, her own daughter the product of rape, she wants only to see her granddaughter safe within marriage.

In **chapter three** Janie marries Killicks, hopeful that marriage might somehow "compel love like the sun the day." It does not, and she turns to Nanny for advice. In Nanny's experience love has always demanded sacrifice—a woman's sacrifice. She advises Janie to be patient, but Janie feels for Killicks only that "[s]ome folks never was meant to be loved and he's one of 'em." Within a month Nanny dies.

In **chapter four**, while Killicks is away, Joe (Jody) Starks a well-dressed, "cityfied" man stops and asks for a drink. More worldly than Janie, he represents to her the possibilities of "change and chance." She leaves Killicks and marries Joe Starks. The reader should consider the implications of marriage in this novel: Nanny had believed that marriage offered protection to her granddaughter. But, the bond seems here to have no legal significance. What sort of protection is possible? Janie's romantic dreams of "flower dust and spring time" cannot endure, as the reader knows, but Hurston's novel is neither an allegory nor a morality tale, and the lessons embedded in the text are not so simple. Joe Starks promises to be "a big ruler of things with her reaping the benefits."

In the **fifth chapter** Joe and Janie arrive at Eatonville, a "colored town," where Starks will establish himself as a civic figure and entrepreneur. Starks astonishes the sleepy town when he pays cash for two hundred acres of land, builds a general store, sells lots to newcomers, and establishes a post office. The idea of "[u]h colored man sittin' up in uh post office" seems preposterous to some, but others sense possibility and progress.

As Starks rightly predicts, the store becomes the natural meeting place for the town. He has Janie work in the store as a symbol and proof of his rank: "She must look on herself as the bell-cow, the other women were the gang." Her silk dress and long, beautiful hair contrasts the humble percale and calico dresses, and occasional "head-rags," of the townswomen. In a scene that draws upon the ideals of ancient Greek oratory, a townsman attempting a panegyric to the Starks is stopped by another who insists that he has forgotten a vital component of this type of speech: He must compare them to the biblical Isaac and Rebecca. All agree that "[i]t was sort of pitiful for Tony not to know he couldn't make a speech without saying that." They appoint Joe Starks mayor and ask for a speech from Janie. Starks intervenes and prevents her from speaking because "[s]he's a woman and her place is in de home." That night he strides home, "invested with his new dignity" and Janie follows, disappointed in her husband, "the bloom off of things."

As Joe distinguishes himself as landowner, mayor, postmaster, and civic visionary, the Starks become separate from the others by class. Many of their neighbors are jealous, feeling somehow as if "they had been taken advantage of. Like things had been kept from them. . . . It was bad enough for white people, but when one of your own color could be so different. . . . [i]t was like seeing your sister turn into a 'gator. A familiar strangeness."

More than the commerce at the store Janie enjoys the conversation, "[w]hen the people sat around on the porch and passed around the pictures of their thoughts for others to see." In **chapter six** "the case of Matt Bonner's yellow mule" becomes a metaphor for the community. The men who sit on the porch of the store never miss a chance to ridicule Matt and entertain themselves with "stories about how poor the brute was; his age; his evil disposition and his latest caper." Janie imagines her own stories about the mule, but Joe forbids her to take part. Joe may believe that her duties in the post office and in the store are her "privileges," but, to Janie, they are "the rock she [is] battered against." He forbids Janie to show her beautiful hair, admired by the men, and insists she wear a "head-rag," which she hates. He cannot admit his jealousy, and Janie compares his reticence to "the matter of the yellow mule."

Joe Starks buys the mule from Matt for five dollars, not to work, but so that the animal can rest at last. The men and Janie are impressed with such a noble act, "no everyday thought." Like Abraham Lincoln freeing the slaves, the power to free the mule makes Joe "lak uh king uh something." When the mule eventually dies all work is suspended. Janie watches from the doorway of the store as "the carcass move[s] off with the town" to the swamp where they "[mock] everything human in death." Joe acts as preacher to speak of "mule-angels flying around . . . [and] no Matt Bonner with plow lines and halters to come in a corrupt." The "sisters get . . . mock-happy" and the vultures circle, waiting for the carcass. The vultures move in, and enact a *mise en abyme*, a play-within-a-play, about the townspeople in the greater human society. When the crowd finally leaves the vultures proceed with mock-human ceremony. None may feast on the carcass until their leader arrives. The "Parson," with all decorum, chants over the mule, "What killed this man?" and the chorus responds, incomprehensibly, "Bare, bare fat." He ritually picks out the eyes and all may then eat.

"The years took all the fight out of Janie's face," and, in the **seventh chapter**, at age thirty-five, she feels beaten down by the routine of the store and by her marriage: "She got nothing from Jody except what money could buy, and she was giving away what she didn't value." Tensions grow between the couple as Joe becomes increasingly sensitive to the contrast between his wife's youthful beauty and his own physical and spiritual aging beyond his fifty years. His body begins to fail him. He frequently speaks of Janie as if she were no longer young. But "[f]or the first time she could see a man's head naked of its skull. Saw cunning thoughts race in and out through the caves and promontories of his mind long before they darted out of the tunnel of his mouth. . . . She just measured out a little time for him and set it aside to wait." Joe humiliates Janie by reproaching her for improperly cutting a piece of tobacco for a customer and, for the first time, Janie challenges her husband in public. "When you pull down yo' britches you look lak de change uh life," she angrily responds. The men in the store laugh and "Joe Starks realize[s] all the meanings and his vanity [bleeds] like a flood. Janie had robbed him of his illusion of irresistible maleness that all men cherish, which was terrible." Joe strikes Janie and drives her from the store.

Joe Starks's death, in **chapter eight**, marks another turning point in Janie's life. She sits alone at his deathbed and pities this man whom she had married twenty years earlier. Although he "had been hard on her and others, . . . life had mishandled him too." Janie removes her head rag and lets down her still-beautiful hair. At once widowed and released, Janie opens the window and announces to the waiting townspeople "Mah husband is gone from me." After an elaborate funeral in **chapter nine**, Janie returns home and burns all her head rags. Self-interested men from great distances come to offer to advise her, telling her, "Uh woman by herself is uh pitiful thing." But Janie likes "being lonesome for a change," and notes that the only difference between her and the many other women like her, is that they are poor and she is prosperous. She remarks to Phoeby that "mourning oughtn't tuh last no longer'n grief."

One afternoon, when Janie is alone in the store **chapter ten**, a stranger, who identifies himself by the end of the chapter as "Vergible Woods. . . . Tea Cake for short," enters and greets her by name, "Good evenin', Mis' Starks." He is from Orlando, seven miles away; he buys cigarettes, and Janie "look[s] him over and [gets] little thrills from every one of his good points." He challenges her to a game of checkers, a popular pastime in the store. She has never learned to play because no one had expected her to do so, until now. When Janie closes the store that evening she is concerned about Tea Cake's long walk back to Orlando. In an exchange that foreshadows her physical and spiritual journey with Tea Cake, he tells her "Ah'm seen women walk further'n dat. You could too, if yuh had it tuh do." He walks her home, she thinks "Tea Cake wasn't strange. Seemed as if she had known him all her life."

In **chapter eleven**, Janie mentally compiles a list of reasons why Tea Cake is an unsuitable match for her: He is "around twenty-five and here *she* was around forty," he doesn't seem prosperous and may be interested in taking her money, and he is "probably the kind of man who lived with various women but never married." She decided to "treat him so cold if he ever did foot the place that he'd be sure not to come hanging around there again." When Tea Cake returns to the store a week later her resolve to spurn him dissolves. Tea Cake remains with Janie after everyone goes home and, at midnight, he takes her fishing. Janie enjoys feeling "like a child breaking rules" and they return to her house at dawn. She "[has] to smuggle Tea Cake out by the back gate . . . like some great secret she was keeping from the town." It is a secret impossible to protect. The difference in their ages worries her and she suspects he may think her a fool. Warmed by his profession of love, one moment she feels "lit up like a transfiguration," only to feel doubt the next. Tea Cake insists that age "got nuthin' tuh do wid love." He is different from any man she has known, "a glance from God." All Janie's uncertainties vanish as they prepare to attend the Sunday School picnic the next day. "You got de keys to de kingdom," Tea Cake tells her, declaring both his love and his commitment to Janie.

Janie's public appearance with Tea Cake at the Sunday School picnic provokes intense disapproval and gossip amongst the townspeople. "It was after the picnic that the town began to notice things and got mad," begins **chapter twelve**. Janie, as the widow of Joe Starks, is a symbol of accomplishment and high class in Eatonville. Tea Cake is a drifter and an outsider. Their catalogue of suspicions and complaints about the pair is long. Nothing escapes scrutiny, from her new dresses and differently combed hair to the certainty that Tea Cake is only after Joe Starks's money. Janie confides in Phoeby Watson that Tea Cake is her chance for happiness, a chance she is ready to take: "Some of dese mornin's and it won't be long, you gointuh wake up callin' me and Ah'll be gone."

In **chapter thirteen** Janie leaves Eatonville with Tea Cake. Those few townspeople who see her board the train for Jacksonville early in the morning note that she "looked good, but she had no business to do it. It was hard to love a woman that always made you feel so wishful." Tea Cake meets Janie on her arrival and they immediately get married. On Phoeby's advice Janie had pinned two hundred dollars inside her shirt, because "[t]hings might not turn out like she thought."

Tea Cake and Janie move into a boardinghouse in Jacksonville and that morning, he leaves early to "get some fish to fry for breakfast." By noon he has not returned and Janie discovers that Tea Cake has taken her two hundred dollars. She remembers another woman, a widow at fifty-two, with "a good home and insurance money." She had love affairs with men and teenage boys, spent all her "ready cash" on them, and was abandoned by each "as soon as their wants were satisfied;" then came a man who persuaded her to sell her house and go to Tampa with him. She was "[a]s sure as Janie had been" when she boarded the train, only to be abandoned by this new man and left to beg in the streets. But Janie is not the fool that the notorious widow was; she has "ten dollars in her pocket and twelve hundred in the bank," and her house in Eatonville.

Tea Cake returns the next day, with declarations of love—and a story about Janie's two hundred dollars. He had "spied the money while he was tying his tie" and pocketed it to count it later. "He never had had his hand on so much money before in his life, so he made up his mind to see how it felt to be a millionaire," and he threw a party to impress old friends and new with his affluence. The account of the party, with an anecdote about ugly women paid not to attend, a fist fight, and Tea Cake retrieving his guitar from the pawnshop converge and collide to diffuse Janie's anger. He promises to repay her by playing dice with the workers who get paid "dis comin' Saturday at de railroad yards."

On Saturday, Tea Cake buys "a new switch-blade knife and two decks of star-back playing cards" and leaves for the railroad yards. Tea Cake returns at dawn, cut in a knife fight when he tried to leave the game; he has won back Janie's two hundred dollars and much more. He insists that she take the two hundred and deposit it in the bank with her own money. He will provide for her from now on, without her assistance. "When Ah ain't got nothin' you don't git nothin'," he tells her. This is "all right" with Janie. As they fall asleep Tea Cake tells her they are "goin' on de muck. . . . down in de Everglades . . . where dey raise all dat cane and stringbeans and tomatuhs. Folks don't do nothin' down dere but make money and fun and foolishness." As Janie watches him in his sleep she feels "a self-crushing love. . . . [and] her soul crawl[s] out from its hiding place."

The richness of the land in the Everglades astonishes Janie in **chapter fourteen**, and the people seem as wild as the lush weeds and wild cane. Tea Cake has come to plant and pick beans and to roll dice. "Between de beans and de dice Ah can't lose," he says. He finds a good job with "houses fuh de first ones dat git dere." He teaches Janie to shoot, advising her that "Even if you didn't never find no game, it's always some trashy rascal dat needs uh good killin'." (Is this remark a foreshadowing of events or is it an allusion to how Tea Cake might be judged by those who do not love him?)

All the workers make money and spend it easily; "[n]ext month and next year were other times. No need to mix them up with the present." Tea Cake's house becomes "a magnet, the unauthorized center of the 'job'." His guitar, his humor, and his ambition draw people to him. People come every night to Tea Cake's house to hear him "pick the box" (play the guitar), to tell stories, and to gamble. Janie laughs to herself, wondering, "What if Eatonville could see her now in her blue denim overalls and heavy shoes?" The men hold "big arguments" like those she used to hear on the porch of the store. But here, "she could listen and laugh and even talk some herself if she wanted to. She got so she could tell big stories herself from listening to the rest."

In **chapter fifteen** Janie learns "what it [feels] like to be jealous" when a young girl lures Tea Cake away from the crowd with games and teasing to make him chase her. Janie thinks that Tea Cake does not resist the girl strongly enough and jealousy, and a "little seed of fear [begins] growing into a tree." She discovers Tea Cake and the girl "struggling" together on the ground between rows of cane, and later, in a violent confrontation with Tea Cake, she believes his denial that he had never wanted the girl. He assures Janie that only she is "something tuh make uh man forgit tuh git old and forgit tuh die."

The picking season ends and most of the workers and families leave. In **chapter sixteen** Tea Cake and Janie decide to stay and work again the next season. Humor and pathos converge in this chapter in the figure of Mrs. Turner, a "milky sort of woman. . . . [who] must have been conscious of her pelvis because she kept it stuck out in front of her so she could always see it." As far as Mrs. Turner is concerned, however, her shape and her features are just fine. "To her way of thinking [her Caucasian features] set her aside from Negroes." She approves of Janie's "coffee-and-cream complexion and her luxurious hair," but despises Tea

Cake because of his dark skin. Negroes are Mrs. Turner's "disfavorite subject." In the face of the woman's earnest fanaticism Janie can think of nothing to say. Janie, conscious of all Nanny had taught her, thinks the woman's speech is "sacrilege" and decides to say no more. At last, Mrs. Turner leaves and Janie finds Tea Cake sitting in the kitchen with his head between his hands.

Chapter sixteen marks the most prominent authorial intrusion into the narrative. Hurston gives to the reader an analysis of Mrs. Turner that Janie would not be able to construct: "Mrs. Turner, like all other believers had built an altar to the unattainable—Caucasian characteristics for all. . . . The physical impossibilities in no way injured faith. That was the mystery and mysteries are the chores of gods. . . . And when she was with Janie she had a feeling of transmutation, as if she herself had become whiter and with straighter hair and she hated Tea Cake first for his defilement of divinity and next for his telling mockery of her." Hurston resumes the story of Janie and Tea Cake with the return of the old crowd for the new season in **chapter seventeen**.

When Mrs. Turner introduces her light-skinned brother to Janie, in an attempt to separate Janie from Tea Cake, Tea Cake has a "brainstorm" about how to assert his possession of her: He "slap[s] her around a bit to show [the Turners] he was boss." The event is the talk of the fields the next day. The men think Tea Cake is a "lucky man" to have a woman who will let him beat her without fighting back. He brags that Janie, although she has money in the bank, will stay "on de muck" in the fields or wherever Tea Cake wants to be. The incident of Tea Cake's slapping Janie disappears into the story. We never learn Janie's response.

The next pay day the men get drunk and, "to take uh rest from our women folks' cookin'" the "familiar crowd" eat dinner at Mrs. Turner's "eating house." Tea Cake, while subtly encouraging a fight among the drunken patrons, acts apparently to stop the turmoil. Another man proclaims Mrs. Turner "more nicer than anybody else on de muck;" she beams on him in approval. But the fight escalates until "dishes and tables beg[i]n to crash." Afterward, the establishment a ruin, Mrs.

Turner angrily tells her husband that they are "goin' back tuh Miami where folks is civilized." Tea Cake has succeeded in driving the Turners away.

In **chapter eighteen** Janie is home alone one afternoon. Large bands of Seminole Indians are steadily moving inland and she learns from them that a hurricane is coming. The people at last believe the signs of danger when "the palm and banana trees beg[i]n that long distance talk with rain." Buzzards gather and stay above the clouds, but Tea Cake refuses to leave because "de white folks ain't gone nowhere" and "de money's too good on the muck." Those who stay wait out the hurricane in their shanties, "their eyes straining against crude walls and their souls asking if He meant to measure their puny might against His. They seemed to be staring at the dark, but their eyes were watching God."

Tea Cake and Janie collect their cash and their insurance papers and wade into the hip-deep water in the yard, amidst fast-moving debris. The ten-foot dike wall breeched, Lake Okeechobee leaves its bed in a two-hundred-mile-an-hour wind. Tea Cake and Janie swim until they "[gain] the fill" where many others also walk, "calling out names hopefully and hopelessly." When Tea Cake is too tired to walk further he "stretch[es] long side of the road to rest" and Janie "spread[s] herself between him and the wind." She is blown into the water when she tries to catch a piece of tar-paper roofing to cover Tea Cake. She grabs the tail of a cow swimming near her, a "massive built dog . . . on her shoulders." As the dog roars and lunges for Janie, Tea Cake dives into the water and seizes the dog, his knife open to kill it. But Tea Cake is exhausted and the dog bites him on the face before dying. Tea Cake and Janie reach Palm Beach in the aftermath of the storm. Janie will never forget the eyes of that dog: "He wuzn't nothin' all over but pure hate. Wonder where he come from?"

Tea Cake is anxious to leave Palm Beach in **chapter nineteen**. But first, he must find work. Two white men with rifles conscript him into "a small army . . . to bury the dead." The white corpses get coffins; the black corpses get quick-lime. He convinces Janie that they must return to the 'Glades. Hurston again intrudes into the mouths of her characters to instruct the reader on racism: "De ones de white man know is nice colored folks. De ones he don't know is bad niggers," Janie observes to Tea Cake. The reader may find it difficult to believe this conversation about something they already know, in a time of hellish crisis.

They return to the 'Glades where there is plenty of work clearing debris to make way for new buildings. Tea Cake buys another rifle and a pistol. He is a little jealous of Janie's skill with a rifle, but proud that he has taught her so well. He soon develops rabies as a result of the dog-bite during the hurricane. The disease has progressed too far for medical help and Janie wishes she had drowned before Tea Cake grabbed the dog: "Tea Cake, the son of Evening Sun, had to die for loving her," she thinks. Suspicions and jealousy become madness in Tea Cake's diseased mind and he levels the pistol at Janie's breast, snapping it once. Janie instinctively brings the rifle around to scare him. He levels the gun at her again, as if "[t]he fiend in him must kill and Janie was the only thing living he saw." They shoot at each other simultaneously and Tea Cake is dead.

Janie is briefly jailed for murder. Because of the circumstances of the killing she is represented, tried, and acquitted (by white men) within hours. She stays at a boarding house that night and overhears men talking: "Well, you know whut dey say 'uh white man and uh nigger woman is de freest thing on earth.' Dey do as dey please." Janie buries Tea Cake in Palm Beach.

In **chapter twenty** the narrative returns to the porch, Janie soaking her tired feet in a pan of water and Phoeby listening to her story. Phoeby goes home to her husband, Sam, vowing to make him take her fishing, and Janie retires to her bedroom. Tea Cake is not dead to Janie: "He could never be dead until she herself had finished feeling and thinking." The killing of Tea Cake suggests that a black woman has an explosive power to claim her voice and to tell her story. ✣

—Tenley Williams
New York University

List of Characters

Janie Crawford Killicks Starks Woods is the protagonist of the novel. Her long, beautiful hair and attractive appearance are mentioned throughout the story. She has a natural and unconscious dignity that often strikes others as aloofness. As a girl, Janie leads a sheltered and conventional life with her grandmother. She is six years old before she realizes that she is black, an event which underscores her isolation from her race and her lack of self-knowledge. Through her first two marriages she holds onto an unrealistic and unfulfilled ideal of love and happiness. In her final marriage, to Tea Cake, Janie is allowed the freedom to be herself, and to love on her own terms. Marriage is the frame for Janie's movement into self-knowledge and maturity.

Tea Cake (Vergible Woods), an itinerant laborer and gambler, is Janie's third husband. Much younger than she, he overcomes her doubts with beautiful language and the expectation that Janie will be herself. He takes a willing Janie into the prosperous farming region of the Everglades to pick beans. He is driven mad by rabies after being bitten by a dog during a hurricane and Janie shoots him in self-defense.

Nanny, Janie's maternal grandmother, is a former slave whose wants only security for her granddaughter. Her life both before and after slavery has been hard; her daughter the product of rape and her granddaughter of a particularly brutal rape which drives her mother away in shame. She lives with Janie for many years in the home of her white employer, the Washburn family. With their help Nanny buys land and a house for herself and Janie. When she discovers seventeen-year-old Janie engaged in an innocent first kiss, she insists that it is time for her to marry Logan Killicks who will, Nanny thinks, protect her from sexual and economic hardship. Love, in Nanny's experience, is "de very prong all us black women gits hung on." Nanny dies believing that money or good white people are a black woman's only protection in life.

Logan Killicks is Janie's first husband. He is much older and owns sixty acres and a house. He loves Janie and is kind to her, but he cannot understand or respond to her romantic ideas in either a mental or a physical way. Killicks is dependable and boring to a young girl dreaming of love. He realizes that Janie does not love him and tries to subdue her spirit by making her do farm labor. She rebels and runs away with Joe Starks.

Joe Starks (*Jody*), Janie's second husband, is an ambitious entrepreneur who takes Janie to Eatonville, a "colored" town ready for development. Soon after the wedding, his talk of love turns to talk of commerce and he buys Janie the best of everything. Janie becomes one of Jody's possessions. He insists that she sell goods at their store or at the post office, and that she wear a "head-rag" to cover her hair that men love to look at. He forbids her to participate in the storytelling that she loves, and he belittles her intelligence at every opportunity. His death releases Janie. She returns to their house, in Eatonville, after the death of Tea Cake.

Phoeby Watson is Janie's best friend, her only woman friend, whom she meets in Eatonville. They love and trust each other and it is to Phoeby that Janie confides her problems and narrates her story. ♣

Critical Views

RICHARD WRIGHT ON THE MINSTREL TRADITION AND *THEIR EYES WERE WATCHING GOD*

Richard Wright (1908–1960), a black American novelist, was also a prominent critic. His criticism combines his love of literature with his passion for politics. Wright joined the Communist Party in the 1930s but became disillusioned with the party in the 1940s, as he records in *The God that Failed* (1950). His novels include *Native Son* (1940) and *The Outsider* (1953). In the following extract, taken from *New Masses*, a Communist newspaper, Wright criticizes Hurston for relying on the minstrel tradition which, he asserts, has plagued black literature and theater since Phyllis Wheatley was writing in the eighteenth century.

Their Eyes Were Watching God is the story of Zora Neale Hurston's Janie who, at sixteen, married a grubbing farmer at the anxious instigation of her slave-born grandmother. The romantic Janie in the highly-charged language of Miss Hurston, longed to be a pear tree in blossom and have a "dust-bearing bee sink into the sanctum of a bloom; the thousand sister-calyxes arch to meet the love embraces." Restless, she fled from her farmer husband and married Jody, an up-and-coming Negro business man who, in the end, proved to be no better than her first husband. After twenty years of clerking for her self-made Jody, Janie found herself a frustrated widow of forty with a small fortune on her hands. Tea Cake, "from in and through Georgia" drifted along and, despite his youth, Janie took him. For more than two years they lived happily; but Tea Cake was bitten by a mad dog and was infected with rabies. One night in a canine rage Tea Cake tried to murder Janie, thereby forcing her to shoot the only man she had ever loved.

Miss Hurston can write; but her prose is cloaked in that facile sensuality that has dogged Negro expression since the days of

Phillis Wheatley. Her dialogue manages to catch the psychological movements of the Negro folk-mind in their pure simplicity, but that's as far as it goes.

Miss Hurston *voluntarily* continues in her novel the tradition which was forced upon the Negro in the theater, that is, the minstrel technique that makes the "white folks" laugh. Her characters eat and laugh and cry and work and kill; they swing like a pendulum eternally in that safe and narrow orbit in which America likes to see the Negro live: between laughter and tears.

—Richard Wright, "*Their Eyes Were Watching God,*" (1937, reprint in *Zora Neale Hurston: Critical Perspectives Past and Present*, eds. Henry Louis Gates Jr. and K. A. Appiah, New York: Amistad Press, 1993), pp. 16–17

✤

ROBERT BONE ON THE ROLE OF SUFFERING IN *THEIR EYES WERE WATCHING GOD*

Robert Bone, formerly the chairman of Columbia University's Teacher's College, was a prominent critic of African-American literature. He is the author of *Richard Wright* (1969) and *Down Home: A History of Afro-American Short Fiction from Its Beginnings to the Harlem Renaissance* (1975). In the following extract, taken from *The Negro Novel in America* (1958), Bone discusses the second half of *Their Eyes Were Watching God* and explores the importance of suffering in the work.

If the first half of [*Their Eyes Were Watching God*] deals with the prose of Janie's life, the latter half deals with its poetry. Not long after Jody's death, Tea-Cake walks into her life. First off, he laughs; next he teaches her how to play checkers. One afternoon he urges her to close up shop and come with him to a baseball game. The next night, after midnight, he invites her on a fishing expedition. Their relationship is full of play, of impulsiveness, of informality, and of imagination. Easy-going, careless of money, living for the moment, Tea-Cake is an incarnation of the folk culture. After a whirlwind courtship, he persuades Janie to leave Eatonville and to try his way.

On a deeper level, Tea-Cake represents intensity and experience. As Janie puts it in summing up her two years with him: "Ah been a delegate to de big 'ssociation of life." Their new life begins with a trip to Jacksonville, "and to a lot of things she wanted to see and know." In the big city, Tea-Cake deserts Janie for several days, while she suffers the torments and anxieties of a middle-aged lover. Upon his return she learns that he had won a large sum in a crap game and had immediately given a barbecue for his friends, in order to find out how it feels to be rich. When she protests at being left out, he asks with amusement, "So you aims tuh partake wid everything, hunh?" From that moment, their life together becomes an unlimited partnership.

From Jacksonville, Janie and Tea-Cake move "down on the muck" of the Florida Everglades for the bean-picking season. Janie goes to work in the fields in order to be with Tea-Cake during the long working day. They share the hard work and the hard play of the folk, laughing together at the "dickty" Negroes who think that "us oughta class off." In this milieu of primitive Bahaman dances, of "blues made and used right on the spot," and of "romping and playing . . . behind the boss's back," Janie at last finds happiness. In true Renaissance spirit, it is the folk culture, through Tea-Cake, which provides the means of her spiritual fulfillment.

One night, "the palm and banana trees began that long-distance talk with rain." As the winds over Lake Okeechobee mount to hurricane force, the novel moves to a swift climax. Janie and Tea-Cake find themselves swept along with a crowd of refugees, amid awesome scenes of destruction and sudden death. In the midst of their nightmarish flight, Tea-Cake is bitten by a dog and unknowingly contracts rabies. Some weeks later, suffering horribly, he loses his senses and attacks Janie when she refuses him a drink of water. In the ensuing melee, Janie is compelled to shoot Tea-Cake to protect her own life. "It was the meanest moment of eternity." Not merely that her lover dies, but that she herself is the instrument—this is the price which Janie pays for her brief months of happiness. Her trial and acquittal seem unreal to her; without Tea-Cake she can only return to Eatonville to "live by comparisons."

As the reader tries to assimilate Janie's experience and assess its central meaning, he cannot avoid returning to a key passage which foreshadows the climax of the novel: "All gods dispense suffering without reason. Otherwise they would not be worshipped. Through indiscriminate suffering men know fear, and fear is the most divine emotion. It is the stones for altars and the beginning of wisdom. Half gods are worshipped in wine and flowers. Real gods require blood." Through Tea-Cake's death, Janie experiences the divine emotion, for her highest dream—to return to the opening paragraph of the novel—has been "mocked to death by Time." Like all men, she can only watch in resignation, with an overpowering sense of her own helplessness.

Yet if mankind's highest dreams are ultimately unattainable, it is still better to live on the far horizon than to grub around on shore. Janie does not regret her life with Tea-Cake, or the price which is exacted in the end: "We been tuhgether round two years. If you kin see de light at daybreak, you don't keer if you die at dusk. It's so many people never seen de light at all. Ah wuz fumblin' round and God opened de door." As the novel closes, the scene returns to Janie and her friend in Eatonville. Phoeby's reaction to the story she has heard is a clinching statement of the theme of the novel: "Ah done growed ten feet higher from jus' listenin' tuh you, Janie. Ah ain't satisfied with mahself no mo'."

—Robert Bone, *The Negro Novel in America* (New Haven, CT: Yale University Press, 1965), pp. 130–32

ARTHUR P. DAVIS ON HURSTON'S VIEW OF RACE RELATIONS IN *THEIR EYES WERE WATCHING GOD*

Arthur P. Davis, formerly University Professor of English at Howard University, was an important critic of African-American literature. He is the author of *Isaac Watts: His Life and Works* (1943) and the editor of *The Negro Caravan* (1941) and *The New Negro Renaissance: An Anthology* (1975). In the following extract, taken from his highly acclaimed survey of black writing *From the Dark Tower: Afro-American Writers 1900-1960*, Davis: American examines some of the characters in Hurston's novel and points out that the lack of bitterness toward whites in the work is surprising.

In *Their Eyes Were Watching God* 〈. . .〉 Miss Hurston tells a moving story of Janie and her search for love and understanding—a love and understanding which she finds, after two husbands, in carefree, happy-go-lucky Tea Cake who is considerably younger than she is. The action takes place largely in an all-Negro town, one like the one in which Zora Neale Hurston grew up—with excursions to the Everglades and to other parts of Florida where Negroes could find work.

The novel develops slowly. One gets the impression that Miss Hurston, like a folk preacher, is feeling her way, reaching for the right mood, which she finally captures. Until she does, however, she fills in with too many tall tales, too much folk anecdote. She, of course, is trying to give the reader the feeling of the talk and the horseplay which take place on the porch of a small-town general store. The objective is valid, but she tends to overwrite.

In Janie, Zora Neale Hurston has created an unusual and fascinating character. Janie, like her creator, is "different"—an unconventional person and the child of a broken home. A light-colored woman married to a dark-colored man, she has the added problems that color prejudice within the Negro group forces upon such a marriage.

In this novel Miss Hurston tells us a lot about the work that ordinary Negroes did in Florida; she also tells us about life in an all-Negro town. One of her better characters is Janie's second husband, the mayor, store owner, and prime mover in this community. He is a new type of Negro character—a wheeler dealer and in everything except color like his counterpart in white novels and white life.

There is, of course, no bitterness toward whites in *Their Eyes Were Watching God*. At the end Janie is forced to kill Tea Cake in self-defense. 〈. . .〉 In the subsequent trial the white judge, the white lawyer, and the all-white jury are all far more understanding than Janie's Negro friends and acquaintances. In short, this is another good-will novel dramatizing the racial philosophy of Zora Neale Hurston—a racial philosophy which present-day black writers would consider incredible.

—Arthur P. Davis, *From the Dark Tower: Afro-American Writers 1900–1960* (Washington, D.C.: Howard University Press, 1974), pp. 116–17

✤

ANN L. RAYSON ON THE LIFE-AFFIRMING QUALITIES OF *THEIR EYES WERE WATCHING GOD*

Ann L. Rayson, a literary critic and author, is an associate professor of English at Lamar University. In the following extract, taken from "The Novels of Zora Neale Hurston," published in *Studies in Black Literature* (1974), Rayson examines the characters and follows the plot twists of *Their Eyes Were Watching God*, describing it above all as a novel reflecting Hurston's "zest for life."

In *Their Eyes Were Watching God*, which happens to be Hurston's best novel, Hurston continues her use of stereotyped characters and plots. The main character, Janie, is Hurston's psychological self-portrait. Furthermore, Hurston's depiction of the various socio-economic levels of blacks reveals her insight into class and caste and demonstrates her ability to project these levels fictionally. Her milieu here is more comprehensive as she moves her protagonist from rural West Florida, to the Negro city of Eatonville, to the Everglades. Each move involves a different man, the last of whom gives Janie her reason for being. Thus, plot, conflict, character, setting, and structure follow the basic pattern, but work together more effectively than in *Jonah's Gourd Vine*. Because Hurston can identify with the heroine, the outcome of Janie's conflict is positive. Janie is real while John Buddy remains a type; her plight communicates itself to the reader.

The novel's action begins with a flashback. Janie, back in Eatonville as an "odd" forty-year-old woman with long hair and muddy overalls, tells her story to a friend. Thus, we first see Janie when at sixteen she is forced by her granny to marry an old farmer with sixty acres, thus prostituting her youth and beauty for Brother Logan Killicks' wealth and position in the community. Janie learns her initial lesson: "She knew now that marriage did not make love. Janie's first dream was dead, so she became a woman." Then Joe Starks, "a citified stylish dressed man," comes along, charms Janie, marries her, and takes her away with him to Eatonville. (Bigamy never becomes an issue worthy of mention.) As Jody rises from store owner to landowner and mayor, Janie grows increasingly disillusioned with her social status attained at the expense of her husband's absence from her. Jody crushes her identity, belittles her publicly. Money and position, social class, destroy the happiness of marriage. Thus, when Jody dies, Janie is ready for the remarkable Tea Cake. She burns her head rags in a gesture of defiance. Other realizations follow:

> She hated her grandmother and had hidden it from herself all these years under a cloak of pity. She had been getting ready for her great journey to the horizons in search of *people*; it was important to all the world that she should find them and they find her. But she had been whipped like a cur dog, and run off down a back road after things.

Then Tea Cake, a genuine good-time man, comes along to teach her to fish, play checkers, pick beans, and make love. He takes her to Jacksonville to marry, then disappears with her secreted two hundred dollars, and inadvertently falls in with good company. He ends up staging a huge, spontaneous barbecue party and returns to Janie twenty-four hours later. She feels used and betrayed only to discover his honest intentions: partying is the staff of life—money is meaningless unless you can enjoy spending it. However, you can also do without it just as well. Consequently, Janie learns yet another lesson from Tea Cake and ceases to worry about money, manipulation, and selfishness. Espousing this philosophy, Janie and Tea Cake are the exception, not the rule. Nancy Tischler explains the significance of Janie's position in relation to its application to black aspirations:

> Her soul needs freedom and experience, not security and power and wealth. But significantly, her search for real values comes after the acquisition of material wealth proves unsatisfying. This cannot become a paradigm for Negro-centered novels until more Negroes have known and reject affluence. To the Dink Britt [industrious drudge] type of dirt farmer, money is the closest thing to heaven.

After this escapade, Tea Cake takes Janie to the Everglades and they earn a living in the groves. In this section of the novel Hurston shows a consciousness of racial oppression. For example, a hurricane destroys the area and Tea Cake is forcibly recruited to dig grave pits for the dead. Whereas the dead whites are at least given pine coffins, the blacks are thrown indiscriminately into ditches. Furthermore, an intergroup racial conflict is introduced by the "color-struck" Mrs. Turner who disapproves of Janie's liaison with the dark Tea Cake. "'Ah can't stand black niggers. Ah don't blame di white folks from hatin' 'em 'cause Ah can't stand 'em mahself. Nother thing, Ah hates tuh see folks lak me and you mixed up wid 'em. Us oughta class off.'" Hurston makes a strong case against this attitude:

> Mrs. Turner, like all other believers had built an altar to the unattainable—Caucasian characteristics for all. Her god would smite her, would hurl her from pinnacles and lose her in deserts. But she would not forsake his altars. Behind her crude words was a belief that somehow she and others through worship could attain her paradise—a heaven of straight-haired, thin-lipped, high-noseboned white seraphs.

Both of these race conflicts contribute to the irony and horror of the climax. ⟨. . .⟩ Zora Neale Hurston probes into the psychology of race, which leads to self-hate based on caste insecurity. Not only do blacks bear the myth of white superiority, but also that of the standard preference for mulattos. Janie is above all such discriminations, yet there is talk of her acquittal for murder being due to her good looks. The aspirations of the landowning farmer and the black bourgeoisie, as represented by Logan Killicks and Joe Starks, are severely criticized as, on the other hand, the simple values, disregard for money and position with corresponding regard for love, unselfishness, and good-timing as represented by Tea Cake, are praised, making *Their Eyes Were Watching God* a novel of *carpe diem*, zest for life.

—Ann L. Rayson, "The Novels of Zora Neale Hurston," *Studies in Black Literature* 5, No. 3 (Winter 1974): 3–4

S. Jay Walker on Hurston's Version of Feminism

S. Jay Walker is the chairman of the Black Studies Program and a professor of English at Dartmouth University. He has published numerous articles in *The Black Scholar, The American Scholar*, and other journals. In the following extract, Walker explores the progress of Janie's liberation in *Their Eyes Were Watching God* and its difference from later feminist ideas of women's liberation.

It is important to note that in one respect Hurston diverges from the radical feminists of the 1970's [in *Their Eyes Were Watching God*]. Janie's search for *people* can only be accomplished through a *person*, a man. In this sense of an individual being incomplete without an individual, personal love, Hurston returns, in effect, to the romantic tradition of reciprocal passion, a tradition as old as Charlotte Brontë and George Eliot, and it is in terms of that tradition that finally she views the relationship between Tea Cake and Janie. Janie herself recognizes that personal love is the cement of her life, and is uncaring that the world will not understand or approve it:

> Dey gointuh make 'miration 'cause mah love didn't work lak they love, if dey ever had any. Then you must tell 'em dat love ain't somethin' lak uh grindstone dat's de same thing everywhere and do de same thing tuh everything it touch. Love is lak de sea. It's uh movin' thing, but still and all, it takes its shape from de shore it meets, and it's different with every shore.

And certainly her love and Tea Cake's is "different." If the apron was symbolic of her life with Killicks and the head-rag of her life with Starks, overalls are the symbol of her life with Tea Cake, for she dons them and goes into the fields to work side by side with him as a migrant laborer in the Everglades.

It may seem a strange "liberation," particularly for the girl who didn't "mean to chop de first chip" for Killicks, but it *is* a liberation; it grows neither out of need nor greed but simply of the desire of Janie and Tea Cake to be together, to share all their experiences, "to partake wid everything," as Tea Cake puts it. And the sharing is genuine: after their day in the fields, Tea Cake helps to get supper. There is no longer the "youse in yo' place and Ah'm in mine" because there are no longer separate places, and it is that blurring of "places," essentially the blurring of sex-role stereotypes within an intensely sexual relationship, that constitutes the liberation and happiness of Janie Killicks Starks Woods. ⟨. . .⟩

As they await the onslaught of the hurricane which is, indirectly, to kill Tea Cake, he questions her about her life: "Ah reckon you wish now you had of stayed in yo' big house 'way from such as dis, don't yuh?" And she replies:

> Naw. We been tuhgether round two years. If you kin see de light at daybreak, you don't keer if you die at dusk. It's so many people never seen de light at all. Ah wuz fumblin' round and God opened de door.

Following Tea Cake's death, Janie returns to Eatonville, still wearing her overalls, to live out her life as she sees fit and to tell her story to her friend Phoeby. There is an ironic indication in the final pages of the novel that Janie, in her own liberation, has become a subversive influence, one that the village arbiters will be hard-pressed to cope with. For, as she concludes her story to Phoeby, her friend, who little more than two years earlier had been one of the strongest backers of the "respectable undertaker" marriage, breathes out shock and admiration:

> Lawd! Ah done growed ten feet higher from jus' listenin' tuh you, Janie. *Ah ain't satisfied wid mahself no mo'*. Ah means tuh make Sam take me fishin' wid him after this. (Italics mine.)

Women's Lib has come to Eatonville, Florida, and Sam Watson, Phoeby's husband, and the other men, will probably find that it takes a little getting used to, just as the world of 1975 finds that the various Liberation groups take a little getting used to.

But in the final analysis, they will probably make it, for as Zora Neale Hurston recognized, the real enemy of progress is not hostility; it is mental inertia, masquerading as hostility or ridicule.

—S. Jay Walker, "Zora Neale Hurston's *Their Eyes Were Watching God*: Black Novel of Sexism," *Modern Fiction Studies* 20, No. 4 (Winter 1974–75): 526–27

ROBERT E. HEMENWAY ON JANIE'S QUEST FOR SELF-DISCOVERY

Robert E. Hemenway is an esteemed critic of African-American literature. He edited and wrote an introduction to *Uncle Remus, His Songs and His Sayings* by Joel Chandler Harris (1982). The following extract was taken from *Zora Neale Hurston: A Literary Biography* (1977). Hemenway explores Janie's quest for self-discovery in *Their Eyes Were Watching God* and asserts that Hurston's view of racial liberation had more to do with developing a cultural awareness than rejecting the surrounding white culture.

Janie's poetic self-realization is inseparable from Zora's concomitant awareness of her cultural situation. The novel also celebrates the black woman's liberation from a legacy of degradation. Janie's grandmother had given wrong directions because of her historical experience; she wants her granddaughter to marry Logan Killicks because of her own slave memories: "Ah didn't want to be used for a work-ox and a brood sow. . . . It sho wasn't mah will for things to happen lak they did." Janie's mother was also born into slavery, the offspring of the master, and Nanny had hoped that Emancipation would bring her daughter freedom. But she is raped by her schoolteacher, and Janie is conceived in the violence. Her mother leaves home a ruined woman, destroyed in spirit. Janie is left with Nanny, who sees the child as another chance: "Ah wanted to preach a great sermon about colored women sittin' on high, but they wasn't no pulpit for me. . . . Ah been waitin a long time, Janie, but nothin' Ah been through ain't too much if you just take a stance on high ground lak ah dreamed." Nanny "can't die easy thinkin' maybe de men folks white or black is makin a spit cup outa yuh." To her, Logan Killicks is "big protection" from this vision; when Janie complains about the absence of love, her grandmother responds, "Dis love! Dat's just whut's got us [black women] uh pullin and uh haulin' and sweatin' and doin from can't see in de mornin' till can't see at night."

Janie has, therefore, both a historical and a personal memory to react against in her search for autonomy. Much of the novel is concerned with her struggle to understand the inadequacy of her grandmother's vision. Tea Cake is not the means to self-understanding, only the partner of Janie's liberation from an empty way of living; she tells Phoeby: "Ah done lived Grandma's way, now ah means tuh live mine." Asked to explain, Janie says,

> She was borned in slavery time when folks, dat is black folks, didn't sit down anytime dey felt lak it. So sittin' on porches lak de white madam looked lak uh mighty fine thing tuh her. Dat's whut she wanted for me—don't keer whut it cost. Git upon uh high chair and sit dere. She didn't have time tuh think whut tuh do after you got up on de stool uh do nothin'. De object wuz tuh git dere. So Ah got up on de high stool lak she told me, but Phoeby, Ah done nearly languished tuh death up there. Ah felt like de world wuz cryin' extry and Ah ain't read de common news yet.

The vertical metaphor in this speech represents Hurston's entire system of thought, her social and racial philosophy. People erred because they wanted to be *above* others, an impulse which eventually led to denying the humanity of those below. Whites had institutionalized such thinking, and black people were vulnerable to the philosophy because being on high like white folks seemed to represent security and power. Janie's grandmother had believed that "de white man is de ruler of everything as fur as ah been able tuh find out." She thinks that freedom is symbolized by achieving the position on high. Zora Hurston had always known, just as Janie discovers, that there was no air to breathe up there. She had always identified with what she called "the poor Negro, the real one in the furrows and cane breaks." She bitterly criticized black leaders who ignored this figure while seeking "a few paltry dollars and some white person's tea table." She once wrote that in her opinion some black leaders wanted most to be able to return from a meeting and say, "No other Negro was present besides me." This sense of racial pride had contributed much to *Their Eyes Were Watching God*: "I am on fire about my people. I need not concern myself with the few individuals who have quit the race via the tea table."

Zora Neale Hurston had spent an entire career chronicling the cultural life of "the Negro farthest down," the beauty and wisdom of "the people"; she did not find racial liberation in the terms of white domination, or selfhood for the black woman in the arrogance of male supremacy. Black people became free not by emulating whites but by building from the cultural institutions of the black community; women discovered an organic relationship with men only when there was consent between equals. This is the key to Janie's relationship with Tea Cake. In their very first meeting Janie apologizes for not being able to play checkers; no one has taught her how. She is surprised to discover that Tea Cake wants her to play, that he "thought it natural for her to play." 〈. . .〉 While Jody would not let her take part in storytelling sessions, with Tea Cake it is perfectly natural for her to be a participant in oral tradition. 〈. . .〉

It is important to note that Janie's participation comes after she has learned to recognize sexism, a necessary preliminary to her self-discovery. In the lying sessions on Joe's store porch, the philosophy of male dominance, often a part of black folklore, was everywhere present. Somebody had to think for "women and chillun and chickens and cows." Men saw one thing and understood ten, while women saw ten things and understood none. Janie eventually informs this male enclave that they will be surprised if they "ever find out yuh don't know half as much about us as you think you do." Her later life with Tea Cake, freely contracted for, without illusion (Tea Cake can be sexist, too), is a natural result of this developing consciousness.

Janie's verbal freedom might not seem such an important matter on the surface, but the reader should remember Hurston's conception of the store porch as a stage for the presentation of black folklore. ⟨. . .⟩

When Hurston writes of Eatonville, the store porch is all-important. It is the center of the community, the totem representing black cultural tradition; it is where the values of the group are manifested in verbal behavior. The store porch, in Zora's language, is "the center of the world." To describe the porch's activities she often uses the phrase "crayon enlargements of life"—"When the people sat around on the porch and passed around the pictures of their thoughts for the others to look at and see, it was nice. The fact that the thought pictures were always crayon enlargements of life made it even nicer to listen to." It is on the store porch that the lying competition takes place, "a contest in hyperbole and carried out for no other reason." Borrowing from the verbal competition over Daisy in "Mule Bone," Hurston uses the store porch as the center of a courtship ritual which provides the town with amusement. Yet "they know it's not courtship. It's acting out courtship and everybody is in the play." The store porch is where "big picture talkers" use "a side of the world for a canvas" as they create a portrait of communal values.

The rhythms and natural imagery which structure the novel refer not only to liberation from sexual roles, but also to the self-fulfillment inherent in this sense of community. Janie's "blossoming" refers personally to her discovery of self and ultimately to her meaningful participation in black tradition. Janie discovers a way to make use of the traditions of slavery—her grandmother's memories—not by seeking to "class off" and attempt to "sit on high" as the white folks did, but by celebrating blackness. ⟨. . .⟩ June Jordan calls *Their Eyes Were Watching God* the "most successful, convincing and exemplary novel of blacklove that we have. Period." She is speaking of Janie's growth into an awareness of the possibilities of love between black men and black women—both individually and collectively, as selves and as members of a racial community.

—Robert E. Hemenway, *Zora Neale Hurston: A Literary Biography* (Urbana, IL: University of Illinois Press, 1977), pp. 236–40

Alice Walker on the Emotional Potency of *Their Eyes Were Watching God*

Alice Walker is a poet, novelist, and critic. She has lectured at Wellesley College and the University of Massachusetts at Boston. She has also been the distinguished writer in Afro-American Studies Department of the University of California at Berkeley and Fannie Hurst Professor of Literature at Brandeis University. She won a Pulitzer Prize and an American Book Award, both for her most celebrated work *The Color Purple*. In the following extract, taken from the preface to *A Zora Neale Hurston Reader* (1979), Walker relates the emotional potency of *Their Eyes Were Watching God*.

Zora Neale Hurston was outrageous—it appears by nature. She was quite capable of saying, writing, or doing things *different* from what one might have wished. Because she recognized the contradictions and complexity of her own personality, Robert Hemenway, her biographer, writes that Hurston came to "delight" in the chaos she sometimes left behind.

Yet for all her contrariness, her "chaos," her ability to stir up dislike that is as strong today as it was fifty years ago, many of us love Zora Neale Hurston.

We do not love her for her lack of modesty (that tends to amuse us: an assertive black person during Hurston's time was considered an anomaly); we do not love her for her unpredictable and occasionally weird politics (they tend to confuse us); we do not, certainly, applaud many of the *mad* things she is alleged to have said and sometimes actually did say; we do not even claim never to dislike her. In reading through the thirty-odd-year span of her writing, most of us, I imagine, find her alternately winning and appalling, but rarely dull, which is worth a lot. We love Zora Neale Hurston for her work, first, and then again (as she and all Eatonville would say), we love her for herself. For the humor and courage with which she encountered a life she infrequently designed, for her absolute disinterest in becoming either white or bourgeois, and for her *devoted* appreciation of her own culture, which is an inspiration to us all.

Reading *Their Eyes Were Watching God* for perhaps the eleventh time, I am still amazed that Hurston wrote it in seven weeks; that it speaks to me as no novel, past or present, has ever done, and that the language of the characters, that "comical nigger 'dialect'" that has been laughed at, denied, ignored, or "improved" so that white folks and educated black folks can understand it, is simply beautiful. There is enough self-love in that one book—love of community, culture, traditions—to restore a world. Or create a new one.

I do not presume to judge or defend Zora Neale Hurston. I have nothing of finality to say of Hurston the person. I believe any artist's true character is seen in the work she or he does, or it is not seen. In Hurston's work, what she was is revealed. 〈. . .〉

I think we are better off if we think of Zora Neale Hurston as an artist, period—rather than as the artist/politician most black writes have been required to be. This frees us to appreciate the complexity and richness of her work in the same way we can appreciate Billie Holiday's glorious phrasing or Bessie Smith's perfect and raunchy lyrics, without the necessity of ridiculing the former's addition to heroin or the latter's excessive love of gin.

Implicit in Hurston's determination to "make it" in a career was her need to express "the folk" and herself. Someone who knew her has said: "Zora would have been Zora even if she'd been an Eskimo." That is what it means to be yourself; it is surely what it means to be an artist.

—Alice Walker, "Dedication: On Refusing to be Humbled by Second Place in a Contest You Did Not Design: A Tradition by Now," (1978, reprint in *A Zora Neale Hurston Reader*, ed. Alice Walker, Old Westbury, NY: The Feminist Press, 1979), pp. 1–3

♣

Maria Tai Wolff on the Symbolism of the Opening Passage of *Their Eyes Were Watching God*

Maria Tai Wolff graduated from a comparative literature program at Yale University where she wrote "Listening and Living: Reading and Experience in *Their Eyes Were Watching God*," for the *Black American Literature Forum*, from which the following extract was taken. Wolff explores the rich imagery and symbolism of the opening of *Their Eyes Were Watching God* and its importance to the work as a whole.

In the opening paragraph of *Their Eyes Were Watching God*, the narrator presents two models for evaluating life:

> Ships at a distance have every man's wish on board. For some they come in with the tide. For others, they sail forever on the horizon, never out of sight, never landing until the Watcher turns his eyes away in resignation, his dreams mocked to death by Time. That is the life of men.
>
> Now, women forget all the things they don't want to remember, and remember all the things they don't want to forget. The dream is the truth. Then they act and do things accordingly.

Men, it seems, stoically watch what reality presents, accepting that which life reveals to them. While they may wish or dream, their inner hopes can be fulfilled only by factors beyond human control; events and circumstances are the "ships at a distance." Men are controlled by Time; if it does not favor their dreams, it will "mock" them, destroy them. "That is the life of men": Life is given, not made. Women, on the other hand, create their own lives from their interpretations of reality. This involves a selective process of willed forgetting and remembering, and it leads to the formulation of a personal image of life, a "dream." On this "truth" of life, women base their actions, living their dreams. Time has less power here; in this process the past is re-shaped and brought into the present, contributing to the acts of the future.

Before introducing the protagonist of the novel, the narrator reveals that this will be a woman's story: "So the beginning of this was a woman. . . ." "This" is the narration of life as lived by a woman, the creation of a "dream as truth." It is also the presentation of a model of reading, of understanding an oral or written text.

Ralph Freedman describes the movement of a lyrical novel as evidencing a "qualitative progression" rather than the temporal progression usually found in a novel. In a lyrical novel, the "fictional world" is "conceived not as a universe in which men display their actions but as a poet's vision fashioned as a design. The world is reduced to a lyrical view." The novel works, then, not as a historical account or narrative of events alone, but as the lyric formulation of a personal vision—or dream. Examining the effects of lyric language on narrative, Freedman writes, "Actions are turned into scenes which embody recognitions."

This transformation of events or actions into elements of a lyrical point of view takes place on several levels in *Their Eyes Were Watching God*. The descriptions of certain crucial scenes, and their repetitions, turn them into emblems or symbols. Yet the transformation of the outside world into a personal vision, of "actions" into self-recognitions, is also the theme of the novel.

A large part of the text is the story of Janie's life; the narrator presents it as Janie tells it to Phoeby. And Janie speaks "full of that oldest human longing—self-revelation." It is she who reveals her past to her friend as she speaks, but, in a sense, Janie also narrates the manner in which her identity has been revealed to her. The story is structured around successive scenes of self-recognition which are Janie's repeated attempts to create a clear, satisfying picture of who she is. The events of the narrative, and the other characters, function within this structure. Janie is led to form her own dream, her own truth, from what she has lived.

Beyond this, though, the text inspires the reader to formulate his or her own personal image of it. The story of Janie is a "revelation" to the reader as well, since the narrative presents a series of perceptions for our evaluation. In hearing, or, indeed, in living, Janie's adventures, the reader is led to re-consider the text within his or her own experience, and to "act and do things accordingly."

The first episode that Janie narrates presents the problem which will structure the series of recognitions in the novel. When she sees herself in a photograph, Janie sees for the first time that she is black. She becomes aware that there are two possible perceptions of her: the intrinsic, natural image she has of herself, and the image held by the rest of the world. In this first experience, the two do not coincide: she says, "'. . . Ah couldn't recognize dat dark chile as me.'" The outside world has also attached its perceptions to her as names, although with no consistency: "'Dey all useter call me Alphabet 'cause so many people had named me different names.'" She is what she has been called. Until a moment just before the death of Joe Starks, Janie will be unable to separate and evaluate these two perceptions, to understand her own identity.

Janie's "conscious life," and the real beginning of her efforts to know herself, begin when she first becomes aware of her sexuality. On the first occasion of this, the narrator, in a lyric passage, uses several images which will recur whenever Janie meets a new suitor. These symbols are the "blossoming pear tree" and the spreading pollen of spring. The perception of these elements in nature responds to certain forces within Janie:

> The rose of the world was breathing out smell. It followed her through all her waking moments and caressed her in her sleep. It connected itself with other vaguely felt matters that had struck her outside observation and buried themselves in her flesh. Now they emerged and quested about her consciousness.

Janie has "been summoned to behold a revelation." These two passages show an essential passivity of her experiences: The world will present itself to her. "She felt an answer seeking her, but where?"

Yet Janie's perception of the world will become an active, transforming one. ⟨. . .⟩

Janie must select from or reconcile material from two different sources: the information about herself she receives from others, and her own feelings and experiences. In a sense, these are two texts, which often conflict. The first, which comes from the spoken opinions of others and corresponds to the "outside" image of her, is almost forced on Janie. The second is less easily explained: It is something she knows and is always capable of possessing, but it must be brought out and valued.

—Maria Tai Wolff, "Listening and Living: Reading and Experience in *Their Eyes Were Watching God*," *Black American Literature Forum* 16, No. 1 (Spring 1982): 29–30

CYRENA N. PONDROM ON MYTHOLOGY AND TEA CAKE

Cyrena N. Pondrom is an associate professor of literature at the University of Wisconsin at Madison. She is the editor of *The Contemporary Writer: Interviews with Sixteen Novelists and Poets* (1972) and *The Road from Paris: French Influence on English Poetry, 1900-1920* (1974). In the following extract, taken from "The Role of Myth in Hurston's *Their Eyes Were Watching God*," Pondrom explores the mythology surrounding the character Tea Cake in Hurston's novel.

Zora Neale Hurston's powerful second novel, *Their Eyes Were Watching God*, has enjoyed—or suffered—a curiously contradictory critical response. It has been praised for expressing the genius of Black folklore and denounced for presenting the Negro as a folkloric stereotype. It has been cited as an apologia for traditional sex roles and praised as one of the earliest and clearest black feminist novels. It has been analyzed as a quest for self-fulfillment or self-identity and as a novel about black love and the humanistic values that love embodies, and it has been both defended and condemned as a novel which expresses its protest against white injustice only by affirming the creative power of black folk life. ⟨. . .⟩

Janie ⟨. . .⟩ acts out a primal order in the universe, and as she comes to understand that order she represents how it should be accepted in human lives. Even before she understands the principles which underlie her longings, she summons men to a primally creative union and wounds them sorely when they fail to achieve its essence. She is again like [the Babylonian goddess] Ishtar, who is both a thoroughly human figure of seduction and the divine force of creation and renewal; the morning and evening star; the goddess of love and war.

⟨. . .⟩ When Hurston introduces Tea Cake, she is at pains to make him the appropriate mythic consort of an avatar of the great female goddess, and an analogue of the dying and resurrected gods. One of the most important elements in this is Tea Cake's youth. The Ishtar-Tammuz, Aphrodite-Adonis, and Isis-Osiris myths are all tales of love between an older woman and a younger man. [Egyptian god] Osiris, for example, explicitly was 28, and Janie, who is "nearly 40" just before Joe's death, is "nearly twelve years older" than Tea Cake only a few months later. Tea Cake, in short, is also 28.

What is more, like those other figures, he is associated with the trees which [Sir James G.] Frazer identifies as among the earliest icons of the worship of a dead and resurrected god. His name, of course, is Vergible Woods (truly, verdantly woods?). And, in a line that recalls Adonis's birth from a myrrh tree, "He seemed to be crushing scent out of the world with his footsteps. . . . Spices hung about him."

Many descriptions underscore Tea Cake's mythic import. "He was a glance from God," Janie thought. After his first night with her, "She could feel him and almost see him bucking around the room in the upper air. After a long time of passive happiness, she got up and opened the window and let Tea Cake leap forth and mount to the sky on a wind." The gesture recalls the sun rising in the morning; when Tea Cake is not there, Janie "descended to the ninth darkness where light has never been." It is not surprising that Tea Cake, like Osiris, is also "the son of Evening Sun."

The freely chosen union of these two, no strings attached, recapitulates the primal act of creation. Janie holds "de keys to de kingdom" for Tea Cake, and he has taught her "de maiden language all over." But this paradisal world cannot remain, just as Ishtar's union with [the god of fertility] Tammuz does not survive beyond the year. The rhythm is fundamental, and inexorable, as birth and death. Working in the fertile muck lands of Florida, Tea Cake and Janie disregard the warnings of hurricane and flood. The waters are already rising when they flee. Seeking to protect Tea Cake, Janie is swept away. When Tea Cake swims to save her, he is bitten by a rabid dog (which could recall Cerberus, guardian of the underworld). Days later, he is overcome by the disease, and he tries to kill Janie in a fit of maddened jealousy. She slays him with an unerring shot, catches him as he falls, and begins her lamentations.

Hurston's text invites a reading of this archetypal scene on levels that are both mythic and social. At the mythic level it is necessary that the sun must set, in order to rise again. The fundamental, female, creative principle of the universe nurtures the corn which much be harvested each year; though its potency is a cause of rejoicing, it must die that human beings may live. The Great Mother/Lover, herself eternal, secures the endless renewal of the earth by seeking again each year a lover who is young and strong. If she is the infinite principle of creation, he is the manifestation of potency in time. But in a world of time, the living age and die. If she is to maintain a "new" world, she must in some obscure way also be responsible for slaying her beloved while he is still in his prime. Her lamentations prove that she loves him still, and in time she calls back the beloved in an endless cycle of diurnal and annual renewal. ⟨. . .⟩

—Cyrena M. Pondrom, "The Role of Myth in Hurston's *Their Eyes Were Watching God*," *American Literature: A Journal of Literary History, Criticism, and Bibliography* 58, No. 2 (May 1986): 181, 192–94

✤

Karla F.C. Holloway on the Narrative Technique in *Their Eyes Were Watching God*

Karla F.C. Holloway, a critic and scholar of African-American literature, is an associate professor of English at North Carolina State University and associate editor of *Obsidian II: Black Literature in Review*. She is also the coauthor of *New Dimensions of Spirituality: A Bi-Racial Reading of the Novels of Toni Morrison*. In the following extract, taken from *The Character of the Word: The Texts of Zora Neale Hurston* (1987), Holloway discusses the role of the narrator in Hurston's novel.

The dialogue in the first sections of Hurston's novels establishes the history and tone of the characters who are presented. In these sections, the characters introduce themselves, interact and set a stage for the events that will occur. Sometimes it is the task of the narrator to set this stage. But the narrative voice in these opening sections does more than simply comment and connect. It seems to take, for this brief moment, a role similar to one Booth assigns the "Outside Narrators," except that this voice is almost like a person, a character standing back and making observations like the one opening *Their Eyes Were Watching God*: "Ships at a distance have every man's wish on board. For some they come in with the tide. For others they sail forever on the horizon, never out of sight, never landing until the Watcher turns his eyes away in resignation, his dreams mocked to death by Time. That is the life of men." For four more paragraphs, this voice philosophizes like a distant and wise observer, and then its vision disappears. Its reemergence is not without this same philosophical perspective that allowed it to say of the people who sit on the porches in late evening that they "made burning statements with questions, and killing tools out of laughs. It was mass cruelty. A mood come alive. Words walking without master; walking altogether like harmony in a song." Except for the fact that Hurston's words do have her as their master, the character of the collected words of her novels is very much like her description above. They are characters because they are words "come alive." The narrative voice that works like this one establishes a relationship within the characters rather than outside of them.

Most frequently, the narrative relationship established with the character who is to come to self-actualization within the course of the story complements this character with parallels drawn between him and nature. It is a choice that grounds the text in African mythology and does so to enable the dialogue of the characters to be surrounded with some measure of the truth that they will eventually come to recognize. Whatever deceit, trickery or ignorance obfuscates the soul, nature remains an image that is constant, truthful and right.

In a discussion of Toni Morrison's novels, Barbara Christian identifies a principle that Hurston illustrates as she structures her narrative voices. Christian writes of the link between the community and nature, a link that is viable in Hurston as well. She writes of "Nature" as a "physical or spiritual force, one that can or cannot be affected by human forces.

For Morrison, as well as Hurston, it is critical for characters to acknowledge the potential of nature, to recognize its role in their communities and to accord it due respect. Not to do so would mean that survival is threatened. Following this perspective we should recognize early that Jody Starks's tearing down the natural environment to erect his town in *Their Eyes Were Watching God* is tantamount to suicide. Hurston was not unaware of this link. The man Janie loved, Tea Cake, followed the land and its cycles as a migrant worker, letting nature and its seasons direct him. Through their imagery, the words in Hurston's novels represent respect for such African valuing of the natural/spiritual world.

—Karla F.C. Holloway, *The Character of the Word: The Texts of Zora Neale Hurston* (Westport, CT: Greenwood Press, 1987), pp. 53–4

✤

Klaus Benesch on the Role of "Black English" in *Their Eyes Were Watching God*

Klaus Benesch is a literary critic and an instructor at the American Institute of the University of Munich, Germany. He is the author of *The Threat of History* (1990), a criticism of Afro-American writers. In the following extract, Benesch explores the role of "Black English," or the African-American dialect, in *Their Eyes Were Watching God.*

At first glance, it looks as if *Their Eyes* is the story of a woman's resistance to male oppression and of her search for identity. If it were not for the abundant use of Black English, which in itself ties the text to a specific cultural background, *Their Eyes* might as easily be taken for the story of a white woman and thus to refer to ubiquitous problems of human existence. Yet, numerous textual oppositions show that there is more at stake here than a confrontation of gender-related interests: oppositions such as people versus things, communication versus isolation, blackness versus whiteness.

Mary Helen Washington argues that "the black frame of reference is achieved in Ms. Hurston's novel in three ways: 1. the language is the authentic dialect of black rural life; 2. the characters are firmly rooted in black culture; and 3. Janie's search for identity is an integral part of her search for blackness." Blackness, represented in the text by the various forms of black folklore and black culture, functions as a kind of barometer for Janie's development. Ultimate emancipation for her means far less to renounce the traditional male-female relationship than to claim active participation in the oral traditions of her environment. It is on the level of language that the reader first encounters this tradition. Dialogue and oral communication are heavily emphasized, and authorial voice, using a so-called standard English, is frequently reduced to a mere introductory function while meaning and content are constituted in the subsequent conversation rendered in a transcription of black rural speech. ⟨. . .⟩ Verbal play and rhetorical improvisation ⟨. . .⟩ dramatize the oral-aural orientation of the black community of Eatonville and demonstrate their linguistic virtuosity, of which

Zora Neale Hurston once said, "who knows what fabulous cities of artistic concepts lie within the mind and language of some humble Negro boy or girl who has never heard of Ibsen."

But Black English and its specific characteristics are also thematically involved in the text. The conflict between Janie and her second husband Joe Starks culminates in an act of speech. As Henry Louis Gates, Jr. points out, Janie not only participates in the rituals of the signifying but "is openly signifying upon her husband's impotency." To Starks's taunting insinuations about her being too old now to mingle with all the men in his shop, she answers with self-confidence:

> "Naw, Ah ain't no young gal no mo' but den Ah ain't no old woman neither. Ah reckon Ah looks mah age too. But Ah'm uh woman every inch of me, and Ah know it. Dat's uh whole lot more'n *you* kin say. You big-bellies round here and put a lot of brag, but 'tain't nothin' to it but yo' big voice. Humph! Talkin' 'bout me lookin' old! When you pull down y'britches, you look lak de change uh life."

After his impotence is publicly exposed, Starks's physical strength declines rapidly. From now on he will not leave his bed, and even the intensive efforts of a root-doctor cannot prevent him from dying soon afterwards. Whether or not his "kidney-failure" is as Gates argues, only a pun of sorts, a hidden allusion to the "actual" cause of his death, to be "kidded" upon, remains unclear. Yet, without doubt, by supplying Janie with the specific technique of signifying at the point of her utmost resistance to banishment from the center of public communication Hurston draws our attention to the preeminent role of oral speech in Afro-American culture. Even more than Langston Hughes, who frequently uses Black English in his fiction and poetry, she emphasizes the cultural autonomy of the Black vernacular, which for her is a language that even the poorest and least educated blacks master and which should not flinch from comparison with any other language, be it American English or the classical European languages. Certainly, when Hurston has Janie remark on the black audience attending her trial—"they were there with their tongues cocked and loaded, the only real weapon left to weak folks. The only killing tool they were allowed in the presence of white folks"—she recognizes the importance of language in Afro-American history, a strategic instrument for both survival and resistance. Yet, by reading/hearing the "voices" of Eatonville it becomes evident that beyond those vital functions Black English has an aesthetic quality of its own, worthy of preservation and cultivation.

—Klaus Benesch, "Oral Narrative and Literary Text: Afro-American Folklore in *Their Eyes Were Watching God*," *Callaloo* 11, No. 3 (Summer 1988): 627–29

HENRY LOUIS GATES JR., ON THE NARRATIVE STRUCTURE OF *THEIR EYES WERE WATCHING GOD*

Henry Louis Gates Jr., the W. E. B. DuBois Professor of Literature at Cornell University, is perhaps the most outspoken critic of African-American literature of our day. His book *The Signifying Monkey* (1988), from which the following extract was taken, won an American Book Award in 1989. Gates examines the tale-within-a-tale narrative structure of *Their Eyes Were Watching God*.

Their Eyes Were Watching God is replete with storytellers, or Signifiers as the black tradition has named them. These signifiers are granted a remarkable amount of space in this text to reveal their talents. These imitations of oral narrations, it is crucial to recall, unfold within what the text represents as Janie's framed tale, the tale of her quests with Tea Cake to the far horizon and her lonely return home. This oral narrative commences in chapter 2, while Janie and her friend, Phoeby, sit on Janie's back porch, and "the kissing, young darkness became a monstropolous old thing while Janie talked." Then follow almost three full pages of Janie's direct speech, "while all around the house, the night time put on flesh and blackness." Two paragraphs of narrative commentary follow Janie's narration; then, curiously, the narrative "fades" into "a spring-time afternoon in West Florida," the springtime of Janie's adolescence.

Without ever releasing its proprietary consciousness, the disembodied narrative voice reassumes control over the telling of

Janie's story after nine paragraphs of direct discourse. We can characterize this narrative shift as from third person, to "no-person" (that is, the seemingly unmediated representation of Janie's direct speech), back to the third person of an embedded or framed narrative. This device we encounter most frequently in the storytelling devices of film, in which a first-person narrative yields, as it were, to the form of narration that we associate with the cinema. ⟨. . .⟩ *Their Eyes Were Watching God* would seem to be imitating this mode of narration, with this fundamental difference: the bracketed tale, in the novel, is told by an omniscient, third-person narrator who reports thoughts, feelings, and events that Janie could not possibly have heard or seen. ⟨. . .⟩

This rather unusual form of narration of the tale-within-a-tale has been the subject of some controversy about the success or failure of Janie's depiction as a dynamic character who comes to know herself. Rather than retread that fruitless terrain, I would suggest that the subtleness of this narrative strategy allows for, as would no other mode of narration, the representation of the forms of oral narration that *Their Eyes* imitates so often—so often, in fact, that the very subject of this text would appear to be not primarily Janie's quest but the emulation of the phonetic, grammatical, and lexical structures of actual speech, an emulation designed to produce the illusion of oral narration. Indeed, each of the oral rhetorical structures emulated within Janie's bracketed tale functions to remind the reader that he or she is overhearing Janie's narrative to Phoeby, which unfolds on her porch, that crucial place of storytelling both in this text and in the black community. Each of these playful narratives is, by definition, a tale-within-the-bracketed-tale, and most exist as Significations of rhetorical play rather than events that develop the text's plot. Indeed, these embedded narratives, consisting as they do of long exchanges of direct discourse, often serve as plot impediments but simultaneously enable a multiplicity of narrative voices to assume control of the text, if only for a few paragraphs on a few pages. ⟨. . .⟩

Hurston is one of the few authors of our tradition which both theorized about her narrative process and defended it against the severe critiques of contemporaries such as [Richard]

Wright. Hurston's theory allows us to read *Their Eyes* through her own terms of critical order. It is useful to recount her theory of black oral narration, if only in summary, and then to use this to explicate the various rhetorical strategies that, collectively, comprise the narrative strategy of *Their Eyes Were Watching God*.

Hurston seems to be not only the first scholar to have defined the trope of Signifyin(g) but also the first to represent the ritual itself. Hurston represents a Signifyin(g) ritual in *Mules and Men*, then glosses the word *signify* as a means of "showing off," rhetorically. The exchange is an appropriate one to repeat, because it demonstrates that women most certainly can, and do, Signify upon men, and because it prefigures the scene of Signification in *Their Eyes* that proves to be a verbal sign of such importance to Janie's quest for consciousness:

> "Talkin' 'bout dogs," put in Gene Oliver, "they got plenty sense. Nobody can't fool dogs much."
>
> "And speakin' 'bout hams," cut in Big Sweet meaningly, "if Joe Willard don't stay out of dat bunk he was in last night, "Ah'm gonter springle some salt down his back and sugar-cure *his* hams."
>
> Joe snatched his pole out of the water with a jerk and glared at Big Sweet, who stood sidewise looking at him most pointedly.
>
> "Aw, woman, quit tryin' to signify."
>
> "Ah kin signify all Ah please, Mr. Nappy-Chin, so long as Ah know what Ah'm talkin' about."

This is a classic Signification, an exchange of meaning and intention of some urgency between two lovers.

I use the word exchange here to echo Hurston's use in her essay, "Characteristics of Negro Expression." In this essay Hurston argues that "language is like money," and its development can be equated metaphorically with the development in the marketplace of the means of exchange from bartered "actual goods," which "evolve into coin" (coins symbolizing wealth). Coins evolve into legal tender, and legal tender evolves into "cheques for certain usages." Hurston's illustrations are especially instructive. People "with highly developed languages," she writes, "have words for detached ideas. That is legal tender." The linguistic equivalent of legal tender consists of words such as "chair," which comes to stand for "that-which-we-squat-on." "Groan-causers" evolves into "spear," and so on. "Cheque words" include those such as "ideation" and "pleonastic." [John Milton's] *Paradise Lost* and [Thomas Carlyle's] *Sartor Resartus*, she continues, "are written in cheque words!" But "the primitive man," she argues, eschews legal tender and cheque words; he "exchanges descriptive words," describing "one act . . . in terms of another." More specifically, she concludes, black expression turns upon both the "interpretation of the English language in terms of pictures" and the supplement of what she calls "action words," such as "chop-axe," "sitting-chair," and "cook pot." It is the supplement of action, she maintains, which underscores her use of the word "exchange."

—Henry Louis Gates Jr., *The Signifying Monkey: A Theory of Afro-American Literary Criticism* (New York: Oxford University Press, 1988), pp. 195–97

✤

JOHN F. CALLAHAN ON HURSTON'S *MULES AND MEN* AND *THEIR EYES WERE WATCHING GOD*

John F. Callahan is a professor of English at Lewis and Clark College in Portland, Oregon. He is the author of numerous articles on American and Afro-American literature and of *The Illusions of a Nation: Myth and History in the Novels of F. Scott Fitzgerald*. In the following extract, taken from *In the African-American Grain: The Pursuit of Voice in Twentieth-Century Black Fiction* (1988), Callahan examines the role of Hurston's *Mules and Men* (1935) in the development of the narrative voice expressed in *Their Eyes Were Watching God*.

Their Eyes Were Watching God is Hurston's novelistic Emancipation Proclamation as, earlier, *Mules and Men* had been her Declaration of Independence from the conventions of anthropology. In *Mules and Men* Hurston applied to anthropology an insight about perception and perspective going back at least to Henry James. She realized, in ways her precursors and many successors have not, that her method of observation and manner of self-presentation influenced the people's (or subjects') expression and revelation of their culture. So she abandoned the premise of impersonal, third-person scholarly objectivity and made *Mules and Men* into a first-person story about her initiation into the practice of fieldwork as well as a collection of the tales she gathered. She became a character in *Mules and Men* as she had been a participant in the black communities of Eatonville and Polk County. Her experience of Negro folklore as "not a thing of the past" but part of a culture "still in the making" mediates between her story and the tales told by her "subjects." Her slowly developing relationships with the people under study and theirs with her authenticate *Mules and Men* both as anthropology and as autobiographical tale.

Mules and Men establishes Hurston's familiarity with the possibilities of first-person narration as well as with the ambiguous implications of the so-called third-person omniscient voice, i.e., what voice, however impersonal in tone or objective in method, can be all-knowing in the face of reality's chaos and contingency? In *Their Eyes Were Watching God* Hurston breathes into her third-person narration the living voice of a storyteller. Implicitly, she puts her personality on the line. For the fashionable value of authorial control she substitutes a rhetoric of intimacy developed from the collaborative habit of call-and-response. Moreover, her performance gives the impression that she is embellishing a story she has heard before, if not from Janie, perhaps from Phoeby, Janie's immediate, responsive audience. Because of her intimate yet impersonal form, Hurston invites her readers to respond as listeners and participants in the work of storytelling. 〈. . .〉

Throughout *Their Eyes Were Watching God* Hurston works out the relationship between her voice and Janie's on grounds of cooperation and support—that condition of intimacy sought by women. Hurston frames Janie's storytelling as a necessary action in the struggle for freedom—in this case a struggle for verbal as well as social equality. To succeed, women must change values, not places, and so authorial control is a false premise, a dead letter in the radical context Hurston and Janie build for the word in the world. Instead of having Janie seize authorial control (a sometimes too simple and arbitrary act in fiction and in life), Hurston improvises an intimate rhetoric of call-and-response. Author and character work together; each shares authorship and authority—collaboratively. Hurston wants to show Janie openly and continuously in the round, both as she sees herself and as others see her. So she calls for Janie's story; Janie responds, and the two women, narrator and storyteller, share voices and perspectives throughout the novel.

As the novel flows along, it becomes "more like a conversation than a platform performance," but Hurston opens with a parable uttered in an improvisatory public voice. 〈. . .〉 Audibly, Hurston declares that the story about to unfold follows from her reconsideration of the old ways of seeing, living, and telling. About men's dreams she is metaphorical in a public, oratorical style. About women she is conversational as if to insinuate her intention to abandon authorial control in favor of a more fluid and intimate style of storytelling. Her voice becomes partisan to women's experience as if foretelling that moment in the novel when Janie realizes that her image of her husband Joe Starks "never was the flesh and blood figure of her dreams," and she begins "saving up feelings for some man she had never seen." Like Janie, the woman, Hurston, the storyteller, has "an inside and an outside now"; like Janie, "she knew how not to mix them" and when to mix them. Like Janie, she is committed to keep the dream alive in imaginative experience. Hurston seeks immensity and intimacy, and from the start, her third-person voice is speculative as well as descriptive, personal as well as impersonal.

—John F. Callahan, *In the African-American Grain: The Pursuit of Voice in Twentieth-Century Black Fiction* (Urbana, IL: University of Illinois Press, 1988), pp. 117–18, 119–20

✣

NELLIE MCKAY ON THE AUTOBIOGRAPHICAL CONTENT OF *THEIR EYES WERE WATCHING GOD*

Nellie McKay is a professor of Afro-American and American literature at the University of Wisconsin. She is the author of *Jean Toomer, Artist* (1984) and the editor of *Critical Essays on Toni Morrison* (1988). In the following extract, McKay examines the autobiographical content of *Their Eyes Were Watching God*.

In Afro-American literature, fiction and autobiography share a long history of common boundaries. Although few would dispute the claim that autobiography has been the preeminent form of writing among blacks for 150 years, all agree that this genre influences and is influenced by fiction, a reciprocal relationship that forces each to greater experimentation. For instance, from its earliest beginnings, by adopting the artfulness and rhetorical structures more usually identified with fiction, black autobiography made of itself a form that signified as well as signified on the totality of the Afro-American experience. Subsequently, complementing each other over time, both have, to their greater advantage, shared similar expressive strategies. As a result, contemporary Afro-American autobiographers are among avant-garde writers in the genre who constantly transgress the narrative boundaries of fiction and autobiography. Thus, in appraising Afro-American traditions in narrative, readers face difficulties when they attempt to separate life and art, nature and imitation, autobiography and fiction. Hurston and later black women writers have taken full advantage of the flexibility of this tradition.

⟨. . .⟩ *Their Eyes Were Watching God* is a representative text in the Afro-American cultural tradition, but one that claims a central place for black women. Writ large, Janie's story reflects efforts by black women, writing and speaking their lives, to liberate themselves and all black people from the oppression of race and sex through the power of language and the struggle to own their history.

In spite of the general agreement about Afro-American autobiography that locates the black self within the racial community, in their personal successes, male autobiographers much more than their female counterparts credit their successes to individual initiative and personal efforts. On the other hand, black women writing of their lives usually see their gains as a result of the support they receive from others with whom they are associated, especially of other women. Hurston's novel goes further than most to reinforce the role of community in this text, which, as Barbara Christian, among others, has observed, is made strikingly clear in the structure of the work. In the mechanism of the story within a story, author Hurston, the critic notes, presented her heroine "not [as] an individual in a vacuum; . . . [but as] an intrinsic part of a community, [to which she] brings her life and its richness, joys, and sorrows." *Their Eyes Were Watching God* is told partly in standard English by a formal omniscient narrator, who is spectator to and participant in the action; and partly in the intimate voice (black dialect) of its protagonist reflecting on her experiences in the presence of a second-person character—the heroine's closest friend, Phoeby, who also speaks in folk language in her own voice, and to whom Janie entrusts her tale.

Further contributing to this understanding of the cultural interconnectedness between Janie's life and her community, Elizabeth Meese finds that Hurston's "method displays a keen awareness of the performative quality . . . that emerges from the tradition of oral narrative, as well as a clever consciousness of the storyteller-writer's role in constructing the history of a people through language." She also observes that the structure of the story, especially considering the role of Janie's friend as chorus/audience, enables Hurston to draw more fully on the "rich oral legacy of black female storytelling and mythmaking that has its roots in Afro-American culture." The writer's aim, Meese points out, is to transform the separate texts within her text into an integrated text; that is, she melds Janie's orality and the narrator's intertexts into a unitary self-contained text that symbolizes "a form of feminist self-definition." The Janie who emerges in this newly formed text represents a harmonious interrelationship among writer, storyteller, and community, as Hurston and Janie, in unfolding Janie's story, change the private autobiographical act into a search for a collective black self that does not negate the importance of her separate parts. The success of this work rests on the harmony of its multiple voices telling stories individually or in dialogue with one another. ⟨. . .⟩

As a professional anthropologist and an Afro-American with deep roots in the cultural life of the folk, Hurston's choice of narrative mode reflects conscious intentions to preserve intrinsic folk forms and values as a vital part of the Afro-American personal identity. But she did not think that in order to be part of the group, one was compelled to sacrifice individuality and freedom from intragroup oppression. As she did in her own life, she permitted her heroine the independence to make decisions, achieve voice, and speak her life as an individual distinct from her community. Still, in relinquishing proprietary claims to the conventional personal narrative, the "I" of *Their Eyes Were Watching God* projects a sustaining connection to the roots of black culture through which her development occurs.

—Nellie McKay, "'Crayon Enlargements of Life': Zora Neale Hurston's *Their Eyes Were Watching God* as Autobiography," *New Essays on* Their Eyes Were Watching God, ed. Michael Awkward (New York: Cambridge University Press, 1990), pp. 54–6, 57

✤

Rachel Blau DuPlessis on Hurston's Use of the Court Trial Metaphor

Rachel Blau DuPlessis, an influential literary critic with a special interest in women's literature, is a professor of English at Temple University. She is the author of *Writing Beyond the Ending: Narrative Strategies of Twentieth-Century Women Writers* (1985), *H. D.: The Career of That Struggle* (1986), and *The Pink Guitar: Writing as Feminist Practice* (1990). In the following extract, DuPlessis explores Hurston's use of a court trial as a metaphor for Janie's trials as a black woman.

The whole narrative [of *Their Eyes Were Watching God*]—Janie's account to her friend Phoeby—is like a trial. The beginning of the novel announces that Janie is being tried by her rural community and condemned without being a "witness" in her behalf, without being asked to testify. The choral collections of folk construct power for themselves through judgment talk, an act that reclaims their humanity despite their being treated as beasts. They scapegoat Janie so they won't themselves be "mules." "Mules and other brutes had occupied their skins. But now the sun and the bossman were gone, so the skins felt powerful and human. They became lords of sounds and lesser things. They passed nations through their mouths. They sat in judgment." This rural gossip, with its combination of paralysis and cruelty (depicted at the beginning in the voices of named black women—Pearl Stone, Lulu Moss, Mrs. Sumpkins—and nameless black men), functionally compensates for the speaker's low racial and economic status; at the same time folk tales/folk talk are extremely vital creations. So this folk talk is presented bifocally by Hurston. It is ennobled by the Biblical and ritualized parallelism of the rhetoric in which she presents these gossips, and folk talk is made inadequate by its sour opposition to Janie's value. Janie, then, undergoes a formal trial by the white community, a second informal trial by overhearing black men's bitter aphorisms on her case, and a third trial by her community of origin. The book involves three trials, one by white people's rules, another by black men's rules, a third by the rules of "Mouth-Almighty"—her black working-class rural community. However, the trial of an autonomous black woman (a black woman who acts equal to anything) cannot play by any of these sets of rules; whatever the judgments rendered, all the trials are inadequate at root. Yet because of the black woman's relative powerlessness, her construction of her own trial by her own rules must be deferred until all of the other trials are finished.

In constructing her story this way—framed thus, and with key moments of undepicted speech to persons who are only partially equipped to judge (although they have various legal and traditional powers of judgment)—Hurston makes the whole story a "retrial," with the proper jury and judge (a black woman—Phoeby), and the proper witnesses and defense lawyer (all Janie herself; note how in political trials, "criminals" often choose to act as their own lawyers). These trials are temporally lively in the narrative choices Hurston makes. The black female trial (Phoeby and Janie) succeeds higher-class white male and female, lower-class black male, and black community trials chronologically, but envelops them narratively. Therefore, Janie's own self-testamentary trial claims final power and final appeal.

⟨. . .⟩ Phoeby's first role is to be the jury of her peers which Janie had long sought for a proper (a telling) judgment of her story. As well she is the next (though undepicted) storyteller or tale-wagger: In a striking image of doubled power, Janie remarks, "[M]ah tongue is in mah friends' mouf," a phrase that means we understand each other so well you could speak for me.

But talk is only one part of power; at novel's end, Janie criticizes those who talk without action: "[L]istenin' tuh dat kind uh talk is jus' lak openin' you' mouth and lettin' de moon shine down you' throat." Phoeby is not one of the actionless—at least according to her self-proclaimed growth and her vow to make Sam take her fishing. But insofar as tales are substitutes for action, the full weight of Janie's final judgment—for she is judge as well as criminal and lawyer—is levied against that displacement. "Talk" in the deep narrative ideology of this novel can be seen bifocally—as folk power, activated knowledge, and judgment possibly motivating action, or as the powerless substitution for both knowledge and action. This bifocal vision of the "talk" of the porch-sitters is a replica of Hurston's contradictory and subtle notions of race: It is a source of power; yet some use it as a shoddy excuse for powerlessness. Thus Janie's silence, insofar as it was filled with "finding out about livin'" autonomously, with learning the necessity "tuh *go* there to *know* there," and with "going tuh God"—a metaphor for extremes of death, love, and suffering—Janie's thinking silence (keeping inside and outside distinct, having "a host of thoughts" not yet to be expressed ⟨. . .⟩ is a source of knowledge depicted as equal to her tale wagging.

—Rachel Blau DuPlessis, "Power, Judgment, and Narrative in a Work of Zora Neale Hurston: Feminist Cultural Studies," *New Essays on* Their Eyes Were Watching God, ed. Michael Awkward (New York: Cambridge University Press, 1990), pp. 105–107

✣

Mary Helen Washington on the Language of *Their Eyes Were Watching God*

Mary Helen Washington is an associate professor of English at Boston Harbor College, University of Massachusetts, and a Bunting Fellow of Radcliffe College. She is the editor of *Black-Eyed Susans: Classic Stories by and about Black Women* (1975) and *Midnight Birds: Stories by Contemporary Black Women* (1980). She was also presented with the Richard Wright Award for Literary Criticism from *Black World*. In the following extract, Washington takes a closer look at the language of *Their Eyes Were Watching God* and looks at the significance of renewed interest in the work.

The language of the men in *Their Eyes* is almost always divorced from any kind of interiority, and the men are rarely shown in the process of growth. Their talking is either a game or a method of exerting power. Janie's life is about the experience of relationships, and while Jody and Tea Cake and all the other talking men are essentially static characters, Janie and Phoeby pay closer attention to their own inner life—to experience—because it is the site for growth.

If there is anything the outpouring of scholarship on *Their Eyes* teaches us, it is that this is a rich and complicated text and that each generation of readers will bring something new to our understanding of it. If we were protective of this text and unwilling to subject it to literary analysis during the first years of its rebirth, that was because it was a beloved text for those of us who discovered in it something of our own experiences, our own language, our own history. In 1989, I find myself asking new questions about *Their Eyes*—questions about Hurston's ambivalence toward her female protagonist, about its uncritical depiction of violence toward women, about the ways in which Janie's voice is dominated by men even in passages that are about her own inner growth. In *Their Eyes*, Hurston has not given us an unambiguously heroic female character. She puts Janie on the track of autonomy, self-realization, and independence, but she also places Janie in the position of romantic heroine as the object of Tea Cake's quest, at times so subordinate to the magnificent presence of Tea Cake that even her interior life reveals more about him than about her. What *Their Eyes* shows us is a woman writer struggling with the problem of the questing hero as woman and the difficulties in 1937 of giving a woman character such power and such daring.

Because *Their Eyes* has been in print continuously since 1978, it has become available each year to thousands of new readers. It is taught in colleges all over the country, and its availability and popularity have generated two decades of the highest level of scholarship. But I want to remember the history that nurtured this text into rebirth, especially the collective spirit of the sixties and seventies that galvanized us into political action to retrieve the lost works of black women writers. There is a lovely symmetry between text and context in the case of *Their Eyes*: as *Their Eyes* affirms and celebrates black culture it reflects that same affirmation of black culture that rekindled interest in the text; Janie telling her story to a listening woman friend, Phoeby, suggests to me all those women readers who discovered their own tale in Janie's story and passed it on from one to another; and certainly, as the novel represents a woman redefining and revising a male-dominated canon, these readers have, like Janie, made their voices heard in the world of letters, revising the canon while asserting their proper place in it.

—Mary Helen Washington, Foreword to *Their Eyes Were Watching God* (New York: Harper & Row, 1990), pp. xiii–xiv

Phillipa Kafka on Gender Roles in *Their Eyes Were Watching God*

Phillipa Kafka is a literary scholar and critic of African-American literature. She is the author of *The Great White Way: African-American Women Writers and American Success Mythologies* (1993), from which the following extract was taken. Kafka explores the use of traditional gender roles in Hurston's novel.

Both Logan Killicks and Joe Starks of *Their Eyes* are men who pursue the masculine success myth, who care only about becoming "great, big men": hollow egomaniacs, incapable of love for anything but outer manifestations of their power. ⟨. . .⟩

In *Their Eyes*, not only do Joe Starks's outward success and economic dreams and goals parallel John Hurston's, his private story does also. His relationship with Janie steadily deteriorates because of his rigid masculinist insistence on gender role playing. This tragedy is the by-product of Starks's adherence to his culture's construct of appropriate male and female conduct in terms of masculine success. For example, both husbands use their wives as reflectors of their success, solely as objects to inspire other men's envy. Their women thus become signifiers for what Thorstein Veblen terms "conspicuous consumption" and what Diane Sadoff terms "gender privilege and gender politics." The more Joe Starks manipulates Janie in this manner, the more their relationship deteriorates. According to Sadoff, "when the radiant attraction to 'horizon' and the feeling of possibility wear off between them, the raw power of sexual domination once more appears in Janie's life."

From Joe's point of view, it appeared this way, according to Hurston: "He saw that she was sullen and he resented that. She had no right to be, the way he thought things out. She wasn't even appreciative of his efforts and she had plenty cause to be. Here he was just pouring honor all over her; building a high chair for her to sit in and overlook the world and she here pouting over it! Not that he wanted anybody else, but just too many women would be glad to be in her place. He ought to box her jaws!"

From Janie's point of view, it appeared another way entirely:

> Jody classed me off. Ah didn't. Naw, Phoeby, Tea Cake ain't draggin' me off nowhere Ah don't want tuh go. Ah always did want tuh git round uh whole heap, but Jody won't 'low me tuh. When Ah wasn't in de store he wanted me tuh jes sit wid folded hands and sit dere. And Ah'd sit dere wid de walls creepin' up on me and squeezin' all de life outa me. [Janie's different interpretation of space after Tea Cake's death is telling.] Phoeby,

> dese educated women got uh heap of things to sit down and consider. Somebody done tole 'em what to set down for. Nobody ain't told poor me, so sittin' still worries me. Ah wants tuh utilize mahself all over.

Unfortunately, over the years, the success myth provides such distractions to the men who pursue it that they lose their sense of humanity and proportion. Joe acquires an "exaggerated sense of 'godliness'" from his success. Hurston broadcasts this to the reader, because every time Joe opens his mouth, he begins with the words "I god." But Janie feels that she has been sold out, not only by Joe, and before him, Logan Killicks, but tragically by her own flesh and blood and sex, her grandmother. ⟨. . .⟩

What is not so clear to readers is that Hurston is pitting women's "love game," against the masculine material "success game," and also against the success game's antithesis, the masculine hedonist who lives only at the beck and call of his emotions. The latter attracts women more than the former, whose obsession for power through material wealth desiccates his ability to love. But the hedonistic man is equally guilty of the sin of pride, of setting the self and its drives and whims above all things.

The misfortune for women attached to such men ⟨. . .⟩ is that they have yielded themselves up to ultimately unbalanced and unnatural men. These women are therefore vulnerable to their men's tendency to make destructive decisions, decisions based on their immediate desires.

—Phillipa Kafka, *The Great White Way: African American Women Writers and American Success Mythologies* (New York: Garland Publishing, 1993), pp. 176, 177–78, 179

✤

Dolan Hubbard on the Mythology of the Black Sermon

Dolan Hubbard, a literary critic and author, is a professor of English at the University of Tennessee. In the following extract, taken from *The Sermon and the*

African American Literary Imagination (1994), Hubbard explores the mythology of the black sermon and its relevance to Janie's struggle to find her voice.

With the spellbound Phoeby at her side, Janie struggles to find her voice and, equally important, an audience that will give assent to her testimony. Janie taps into the responsive mythology of the black sermon as she assigns meaning to her experience. She exercises autonomy in making her world through language. However, while the language of the black church provides her one means of translating Janie's experience into a medium that can be comprehended easily by a member of her aesthetic community, Hurston keeps before us the inescapable fact that the community acts upon Janie, and Janie upon the community. She differs from her community in that her action is a break from gendered silence.

The logical conclusion to Janie's female-centered discourse occurs when Phoeby, who aspires "to sit on de front porch," undergoes a transformation. With the exhilaration that only the newly converted can know, Phoeby enthusiastically becomes Janie's disciple: "'Lawd!' Phoeby breathed out heavily, 'Ah done growed ten feet higher from jus' listenin' tuh you, Janie. Ah ain't satisfied wid mahself no mo'. Ah means tuh make Sam take me fishin' wid him after this. Nobody [i.e., the negative community of women and the signifying men] better not criticize yuh in mah hearin'.'" Phoeby responds excitedly to Janie's call to break with hierarchies of representations and to stop seeing herself as a silent subject. It is significant to point out that Janie comes to Phoeby religiously speaking, from a point of strength, not coping. She knows who her God is. She does not seek confirmation for her actions, but affirmation of voice. The religious imagination of the community enters into Janie's verbal consciousness and shapes her response to historical pressures.

The language of the black church is a communal language invested with authority. Not only does this communal language give Janie voice and legitimacy, but it also sustains her. Through it, she can prevent the memory of Tea Cake from dying. The connection to romance—a vertical language—becomes apparent to the mesmerized Phoeby as well as to the reader-participant. Janie's ritual retelling of her journey toward the horizon enables her to suspend her rules of time and space as she moves toward the climactic moment in her sermon—the tragic death of her beloved Tea Cake. Each time Janie tells of their short but intense life together, she relives the experience, much as Christians do when they participate in the Eucharist. In fact *Their Eyes Were Watching God* may be viewed as a series of revelations leading toward ultimate revelation—Janie's being reunited in the spirit with Tea Cake.

The novel ends where it began, within the perceptual field of the narrator, who releases it from the temporal world. In this way, Janie and Tea Cake achieve a greater freedom in the world tomorrow, and Janie triumphs over her critics, the negative community of gossiping women to whom the reader is introduced in the book's opening sequence. With her spiritual loyalties no longer divided, Janie, in a picture at least as arresting as the novel's opening scene, draws the various strands of her sermon together: "She pulled in her horizon like a great fish-net. Pulled it from around the waist of the world and draped it over her shoulder. So much of life in its meshes! She called in her soul to come and see." In pulling the fishnet around her shoulder, Janie arrests the "eschatological despair." An optimist and a romantic, Janie seeks a larger space for herself and her life's story; her quest involves woman's timeless search for freedom and wholeness. Her charge to her new convert is "you got tuh *go* there tuh *know* there." Janie, in her movement toward the horizon (i.e., the successful execution of her performance via the sermon), is transformed from blues figure to prophet. In moving toward this transformation, she both achieves personal fulfillment and assumes a communal role traditionally reserved for males. She appropriates tropes of creation ("She had given away everything in their little house except a package of garden seed that Tea Cake had bought to plant") and reunion ("She pulled in her horizon like a great fish-net") in order to insert her voice into history.

In the end, Janie's sermon becomes a poetry of affirmation—with self, community, and loved ones. Janie and Phoeby are uplifted through the preached word. Operating from a position of strength within the ethos of her community, Janie achieves an unspeakable intimacy that bonds her to her community of faith.

—Dolan Hubbard, *The Sermon and the African American Literary Imagination* (Columbia: University of Missouri Press, 1994), pp. 62–3

✣

KIMBERLY RAE CONNOR ON JANIE'S GUIDES TOWARD SELF-AWARENESS

Kimberly Rae Connor is a literary critic and the author of *Conversions and Visions in the Writings of African-American Women* (1994), from which the following extract was taken. Connor explores the roles of Tea Cake, Mrs. Turner, and the Christian God in guiding Janie toward an understanding of herself and the world around her.

Janie and Tea Cake pledge to do as much as they can together. They move to Florida and work together harvesting beans in "the muck." Their home becomes the center of the community, like a storefront porch, because of the energy and enthusiasm they create together. They do not live off of Janie's wealth but "live offa happiness." At this point in the narrative Hurston displays her anthropological gifts, conveying the life of Janie and Tea Cake in vivid folklore images, once again establishing the importance and primacy of this mode of living and seeing. One sees storytelling rendered for its own sake and one hears the stories of the "big picture talkers," who use "a side of the world for a canvas." Janie learns to "tell big stories," and indeed the story she tells Phoeby is an example of the ability and vision she has acquired. With Tea Cake as her guide, Janie explores the soul of her culture and learns how to value herself within this context. Although it was by challenging her grandmother's vision that Janie understood herself as different from cultural prescription, it is through Tea Cake that she comes to view herself as culturally defined. Both modes of self-discovery are essential, however, and both reflect the reliance on others, on community, that is so characteristic of African-American culture.

Yet it is on the muck that Janie also meets Mrs. Turner, who has "built an altar to the unattainable" and whose perverted sense of being is all tied up in illusory images. Her God, unlike Janie's "demands blood" and inspires fear. Mrs. Turner is drawn to Janie because of her light complexion and tries to turn her against the darker Tea Cake. Her influence poisons even Tea Cake, who, in an effort to show "who's boss," beats Janie. Mrs. Turner misses what Janie sees—a sacrality in herself as created by God and loved by Tea Cake. Just as there is a God to watch, to turn to for answers and help, so too are there false gods who need watching.

When the hurricane hits the Everglades, all "eyes were questioning God." Janie and Tea Cake reflect on death, and Tea Cake, who worries for the peril in which he may have placed Janie, is reassured by her with these words: "If you kin see de light at daybreak, you don't keer if you die at dusk. It's so many people never seen de light at all. Ah wuz fumblin' round and God opened de door." As Sigrid King notes, God becomes "a name for what she has learned through her own growth and through her relationship with Tea Cake. God is the unexplainable force which Janie is constantly seeking." Janie reestablishes a self-authenticated concept of living in theological terms that dictate the kind of life one leads rather than the length of one's life. Those who may think they are alive, the unconverted, are not really living until they embrace self and life's full potential. The hurricane comes to take on an almost apocalyptic symbolic significance as living and dead are inverted by the storm—inanimate objects tossed into animate motion, living things crushed and rendered lifeless by the waves. It is in this context that Tea Cake's death occurs. As he lay dying from the bite of a rabid dog, Janie

> looked hard at the sky for a long time. Somewhere up there beyond blue ether's bosom sat He. Was He noticing what was going on around here? He must be because He knew everything. Did he mean to do this thing to Tea Cake and her? It wasn't anything she could fight. She could only ache and wait. Maybe it was some big tease and when He saw it had gone far enough He'd give her a sign. She looked hard for something up

there to move for a sign. A star in the daytime, maybe, or the sun to shout, or even a mutter of thunder. Her arms went up in a desperate supplication for a minute. It wasn't exactly pleading, it was asking questions. The sky stayed hard looking and quiet so she went inside the house. God would do less than He had in His heart.

Janie neither strains for help from God nor rages over his doing "less than He had in His heart," because God has been her companion through her changes. He has given her the knowledge no one else could, and he was also the one who brought her to Tea Cake: "Ah jus' know dat God snatched me out de fire through you." When she must shoot Tea Cake in self-defense, Janie calls it "the meanest moment of eternity" yet knows too that "no hour is ever eternity, but it has its right to weep," a sentiment that recalls Nanny's comment that "folks meant to cry 'bout somethin' or other." So she thanks Tea Cake for the chance for "loving service." Tea Cake has given her the opportunity to appreciate her own self-worth, a quality necessary to live alone without him. Her own transcendent vision can now expand on reality rather than denying it.

—Kimberly Rae Connor, *Conversions and Vision in the Writings of African-American Women* (Knoxville, TN: University of Tennessee Press, 1994), pp. 158–60

✤

John Lowe on Freud's Concept of Humor as an Aggressive Force and *Their Eyes Were Watching God*

John Lowe has taught at Harvard University where he was the Andrew W. Mellon Fellow in African-American Studies. He is currently an associate professor of English at Louisiana State University where he teaches African-American, Southern, and ethnic literature and theory. In the following extract, taken from *Jump at the Sun: Zora Neale Hurston's Cosmic Comedy* (1994), Lowe uses Freud's concept of humor as an aggressive force to examine the comic scenes in *Their Eyes Were Watching God.*

Henry Louis Gates, Jr., in *The Signifying Monkey* provides an intriguing reading of *Their Eyes*, demonstrating Hurston's success in creating what he calls a "speakerly text," which introduces free indirect discourse into African American narration. Doing so enables her to gradually annul the distance between her own authorial voice and those of her characters, especially Janie's, a device that enables the intimacy of first person narration while avoiding its restrictions. The speakerly text privileges its own folk-centered, vernacular mode of narration over all other structural elements. Gates does especially well in linking signification with the pattern of play and gaming in the novel, although after touching on this he goes on to his real interest, Hurston's narrative play. I would add that humor constitutes a key ingredient in Hurston's craft and especially in the play aspect that so intrigues Gates. Dialect, after all, finds its shape and form from folk content, and humor functions as the heart and soul of both Hurston's idiomatic prose and presentations of play.

Hurston signals the importance of Janie's linguistic maturity by emphasizing through the frame story the verbal tools she bears within her as she marches back into Eatonville at the opening of the novel. In this respect she proves fortuitously armed, for the community has an arsenal of scorn waiting for her: "Seeing the woman as she was made them remember the envy they had stored up and swallowed with relish. They made burning statements with questions, and killing tools out of laughs." This returns us with a vengeance to Freud's concept of humor as an aggressive force. Their cruel laughter has a base in presumed dichotomies, always a rich source of mirth; the blue satin dress of her departure against the overalls of her return, the money left by Jody and the money now presumed squandered, the woman of forty with the loose hair of "some young gal," but most of all, the woman of forty alone, not the woman who left with "dat young lad of a boy." Janie, they hope, will turn out to be a comic script they know well and hope to use, for they intend their humor to "uncrown" Janie, as Bakhtin would say, to make her "fall to their level." The women hoard up this image, knowing they might need it, for their men are also "reading" this text, seeing Janie's "firm buttocks like she had grape fruits in her hip pockets" and her "pugnacious breasts trying to bore holes in her shirt." A comic contrast develops between the men's richly appreciative and sly appraisal of the body and the women's smugly snickering scorn, but both depersonalize her. After Janie wordlessly enters her gate and slams it behind her, "Pearl Stone opened her mouth and laughed real hard because she didn't know what else to do." Like Hester Prynne in the opening pages of *The Scarlet Letter*, Janie will be the victim of cruel, unthinking humor until she silences it, and unlike Hester, she must cap the discussion by having the last laugh herself. 〈. . .〉

Back in Eatonville, Janie has to "make her case" among her people, with their involvement. Individual achievement finds its ultimate fulfillment in conjunction with others, and as Mary Helen Washington wisely observes, "the deepest and most lasting relationships occur among those black people who are most closely allied with and influenced by their own community" (*Black-Eyed* xxx). Janie instinctively knows that she can find peace only when the story untold at the trial becomes lodged in the figurative bosom and collective memory of her home community. The telling of her story, in the people's own loving, laughing voice, confirms its communal, cultural relevance, assures its immortality, and embalms her love for Tea Cake.

Throughout *Their Eyes Were Watching God* Hurston indicates that in refusing one's heritage, a person commits cultural suicide, and the loss of laughter represents an early symptom of that internal death. In a unique way, both Janie Crawford Killicks Starks Woods and Zora Neale Hurston recognized and harnessed humor's powerful resources; using its magical ability to bring people together, they established the intimacy of democratic communion.

On the other hand, Washington has also warned us against reading this novel too positively, for Janie indeed is silenced at any number of places, and we have no assurance that her voice will reverberate in the community again beyond the telling of her story through Phoeby. Janie herself issues a qualification as she summarizes the buzzing curiosity and gossiping of the townspeople to Phoeby: "'Dem meatskins is *got* tuh rattle tuh make out they's alive. Let 'em consolate theyselves wid talk. 'Course, talkin' don't amount tuh uh hill uh beans when yuh can't do nothin' else. And listenin' tuh dat kind uh talk is jus' lak openin' you' mouth and lettin' de moon shine down yo' throat. ⟨. . .⟩ Two things everybody's got tuh do fuh theyselves. They got tuh go tuh God, and they got tuh find out about livin' fuh theyselves.'" Ultimately, as this passage suggests, language itself becomes limited, unable to reach what Hurston calls that "gulf of formless feelings untouched by thought." People thus need the other arts and any other feeble tool they can create to assault the voids of silence that divide us.

Humor, I would suggest, springs from the failures of ordinary, standard language to adequately communicate human needs, emotions, and expressions. It offers an expansion of language that goes even beyond metaphor. Indeed, as Hurston indicates in "Characteristics of Negro Expression," humorous gestures can function as communication, displacing and frequently transcending the limitations of spoken or written discourse. Comic creation of all types, however, paints, as Hurston might say, a "hieroglyphics" of mirth, speaking to us in a way that unadorned speech never can, moving us as close as language can ever get to what Janie instinctively understands as "the inaudible voice of it all."

—John Lowe, *Jump at the Sun: Zora Neale Hurston's Cosmic Comedy* (Urbana, IL: University of Illinois Press, 1994), pp. 158-59, 197–98

✣

Works by Zora Neale Hurston

Jonah's Gourd Vine. 1934.

Mules and Men. 1935.

Their Eyes Were Watching God. 1937.

Tell My Horse. 1938.

Moses, Man of the Mountain. 1939.

Dust Tracks on a Road. 1942.

Seraph on the Suwanee. 1949.

I Love Myself When I Am Laughing . . . & Then Again When I Am Looking Mean and Impressive: A Zora Neale Hurston Reader. Ed. Alice Walker. 1979.

The Sanctified Church. Ed. Toni Cade Bambara. 1981.

Spunk: The Selected Short Stories of Zora Neale Hurston. 1985.

Works About Zora Neale Hurston and *Their Eyes Were Watching God*

Awkward, Michael. *Inspiring Influences: Tradition, Revision, and Afro-American Women Novelists*. New York: Columbia University Press, 1989.

Baker, Houston A., Jr. *Blues, Ideology, and Afro-American Literature: A Vernacular Theory*. Chicago: University of Chicago Press, 1984.

Bethel, Lorraine. "'This Infinity of Conscious Pain'": Zora Neale Hurston and the Black Female Literary Tradition," *But Some of Us Are Brave*, ed. Gloria T. Hull, Patricia Bell Scott, and Barbara Smith. Old Westbury, NY: The Feminist Press, 1982, pp. 176–88.

Bloom, Harold, ed. *Zora Neale Hurston*. New York: Chelsea House, 1986.

———. *Zora Neale Hurston's "Their Eyes Were Watching God."* New York: Chelsea House, 1987.

Brawley, Benjamin. *The Negro Genius*. New York: Biblio & Tannen, 1966.

Brown, Lloyd W. "Zora Neale Hurston and the Nature of Female Perception," *Obsidian* 4 (Winter 1978), pp. 39–45.

Brown, Sterling. "Luck is a Fortune," *Nation* 145, No. 6 (October 16, 1937), pp. 409–10.

Byrd, James W. "Zora Neale Hurston: A Novel Folklorist," *Tennessee Folklore Society Bulletin* 21 (1955), pp. 37–41.

Christian, Barbara. *Black Women Novelists: The Development of a Tradition 1892–1976*. Westport, CT: Greenwood Press, 1980.

Cooke, Michael G. *Afro-American Literature in the Twentieth Century: The Achievement of Intimacy*. New Haven, CT: Yale University Press, 1984.

Giles, James R. "The Significance of Time in Zora Neale Hurston's *Their Eyes Were Watching God*," *Negro American Literature Forum* 6 (Summer 1972), pp. 52–53, 60.

Gloster, Hugh M. *Negro Voices in American Fiction*. New York: Russell & Russell, 1966.

Hill, Lynda Marion. *Social Rituals and the Verbal Art of Zora Neale Hurston*. Washington, DC: Howard University Press, 1996.

Holt, Elvin. "Zora Neale Hurston," *Fifty Southern Writers After 1900*, ed. Joseph M. Flura and Robert Bain. Westport, CT: Greenwood Press, 1987, pp. 259–69.

Howard, Lillie. *Zora Neale Hurston*. Boston: G. K. Hall, 1980.

———. "Nanny and Janie: Will the Twain Ever Meet?," *Journal of Black Studies* 12 (Winter 1982), pp. 403–14.

Howard, Lillie, ed. *Alice Walker and Zora Neale Hurston: The Common Bond*. Westport, CT: Greenwood Press, 1987, pp. 259–69.

Johnson, Barbara. "Metaphor, Metonymy, and Voice in Their Eyes," *Black Literature and Literary Theory*, ed. Henry Louis Gates Jr. New York: Methuen, 1984, pp. 205–21.

———. *A World of Difference*. Baltimore: Johns Hopkins University Press, 1987.

Jordan, Jennifer. "Feminist Fantasies: Zora Neale Hurston's *Their Eyes Were Watching God*," *Tulsa Studies in Women's Literature* 7 (Spring 1988), pp. 105–17.

Jordan, June. "On Richard Wright and Zora Neale Hurston," *Black World* 23 (August 1974), pp. 4–8.

Kubitsch, Missy Dehn. "'Tuh De Horizon and Back': The Female Quest in *Their Eyes Were Watching God*," *Black American Literature Forum* 17 (Fall 1983), pp. 109–15.

Lupton, Mary Jane. "Zora Neale Hurston and the Survival of the Female," *Southern Literary Journal* 15 (Fall 1982), pp. 25–8.

Sigglow, Janet Carter. *Making Her Way with Thunder: A Reappraisal of Zora Neale Hurston's Narrative Art*. New York: P. Lang, 1994.

Spillers, Hortense J. "A Hateful Passion, A Lost Love," *Feminist Issues in Literary Scholarship*, ed. Shari Benstock. Bloomington: Indiana University Press, 1987, pp. 181–287.

Stepto, Robert. *From Behind the Veil: A Study of Afro-American Narrative*. Urbana: University of Illinois Press, 1979.

Walker, Alice. "In Search of Zora Neale Hurston," *Ms.* (March 1975), pp. 74–79, 95–89.

———. *In Search of Our Mother's Gardens: Womanist Prose*. San Diego: Harcourt Brace Jovanovich, 1983.

Wall, Cheryl. *Women of the Harlem Renaissance*. Bloomington: Indiana University Press, 1995.

Wallace, Michele. "'Who Day Say Who Dat When I Say Who Dat?': Zora Neale Hurston Then and Now," *The Village Voice Literary Supplement* (April 1988), pp. 18–21.

Weizlmann, Joe and Houston A. Baker Jr. eds. *Studies in Black American Literature 3: Black Feminist Criticism and Critical Theory*. Greenwood, FL: Penkvill Publishing, 1988.

Willis, Miriam. "Folklore and the Creative Artist: Lydia Cabrera and Zora Neale Hurston," *CLA Journal* 27 (September 1983), pp. 81–89.

Willis, Susan. *Specifying: Black Women Writing the American Experience*. Madison: University of Wisconsin Press, 1987.

Index of Themes and Ideas

BONNER, MATT, and his role in the novel, 16–17

COMMUNITY, role of in novel, 59–60, 74

GENDER ROLES, in novel, 13, 40, 43–44, 48, 65–67

GOD, Janie's self-awareness and, 71–72

HUMOR, role of in novel, 72–75

HURSTON, ZORA NEALE: black female singers and, 42; heroic vitalism in, 9–10; life of, 11–12

KILLICKS, LOGAN: and his role in the novel, 14, 15, 25, 26, 33, 35, 36, 38; success myth and, 67

MARRIAGE, implications of in novel, 15

MULE, as metaphor, 16–17

MULES AND MEN: narrative voice in, 56–58; signifying in, 55

NANNY, and her role in the novel, 9, 14–15, 22, 25, 38, 41, 67, 72

PORCH, as symbol, 40, 54, 63, 68

STARKS, JOE (JODY): Black English and, 52; death of, 17–18, 28; and his role in the novel, 32, 33, 35, 36, 39, 40, 45, 50, 58, 66, 67; success myth and, 66, 67

TAYLOR, "SHIFTLESS" JOHNNY, and his role in the novel, 14

TEA CAKE (VERGIBLE WOODS), and his role in the novel, 9–10, 13, 18–24, 25, 26, 27, 28–29, 31, 33–34, 35–36, 38, 39, 40, 50, 53, 64–65, 69, 72, 74; Janie's self-awareness and, 70–71, 72; killing of, 24, 27, 29–30, 32, 36, 48, 69, 72; as mythic consort for Janie, 46–48

THEIR EYES WERE WATCHING GOD: as autobiography, 32, 59–60, 65–67; as *Bildungsroman*, 14; Black English in, 13, 42, 51–53, 60; as court trial, 32, 35, 52, 61–63; emotional potency of, 41–43; gender roles in, 13, 40, 43–44, 48, 65–67; humor in, 72–75; life-affirming qualities of, 32–35; as lyrical novel, 44, 45; male-dominated literary canon revised by, 64–65; metaphor in, 13, 16, 39; minstrel tradition in, 27–28; narrative technique of, 49–50, 53–58, 60–61; opening of, 43–46, 49; race as element in, 23–24, 27–28, 31–32, 34–35, 37–41; as sexist, 35–37; signifying in, 55–56, 66; storyteller's voice in, 13, 56–58, 60; suffering in, 28–30; tale-within-a-tale narrative structure of, 53–56, 60; thematic and structural analysis of, 13–24

TREE, as *motif*, 14, 45, 47

TURNER, MRS.: and her role in the novel, 21–23, 34; Janie's self-awareness and, 71

WATSON, PHOEBE: and her role in the novel, 13, 18, 19, 24, 26, 36–37, 38, 44, 53, 54, 57, 60, 65, 68, 69, 70, 74; as judge and jury, 62–63

WATSON, SAM, and his role in the novel, 24, 37, 63, 68

WOODS, JANIE CRAWFORD KILLICKS STARKS: as autobiographical, 32; awareness of self and, 14, 20, 37–41, 44–45, 70–72; Black English and, 52; epiphany of, 14, 45; heroic vitalism in, 9–10; and her role in the novel, 13, 14–15, 16–24, 25, 26, 27, 29–33, 34, 35, 39, 47, 48, 53, 54, 55, 57, 60, 64–65, 66–67; humor and, 72–75; liberation of, 35–41, 57–58; story of as trial, 32, 35, 52, 61–63; struggle of as African American church sermon, 67–70; tragic intensity of, 28–30; transformative power of, 24, 43–46